ADAM: WHO IS HE?

ADAM
WHO IS HE?

Mark E. Petersen

Published by
Deseret Book Company
Salt Lake City, Utah
1976

CONTENTS

OUR
CERTAIN
GUIDE

We accept the ancient and modern scriptures as the word of God. They are our unerring guides. But some teach doctrines contrary to the scripture. Under these circumstances it is well to remember President Joseph Fielding Smith, who said: "If I ever say anything contrary to the scriptures, the scriptures prevail." It is so with everyone.

It is hoped that this book will be read with that choice bit of wisdom in mind.

Chapter One

SUBJECTS
OF DEBATE

Adam, the first man, is a controversial figure in the minds of many people. So is Eve, his wife. Together, they probably are the most misunderstood couple who ever lived on the earth.

This is hardly to be wondered at, though. Misconceptions and far-out theories have been bombarding the public concerning our first parents for centuries past. Probably the most to blame are teachers of religion themselves. Not knowing the facts about Adam and Eve, they have foisted their own private notions and uninspired creeds upon the people, with the result that a mass of confusion has mounted year after year.

Their doctrine concerning original sin has been at the root of most of the trouble. But the more recent tendency of clergymen and scholars alike to call the Garden of Eden account in the Bible a mere myth has not helped the situation. Neither have the evolutionary theories that attempt to trace our pedigrees back to some accidental development of a single cell which, it is alleged, eventually became human.

Adding to the confusion are some who have so completely misunderstood gospel truths concerning the Garden of Eden that they assume that Adam was Deity, a thing completely at variance with both ancient scripture and modern revelation.

Some Jewish scholars also have joined the parade by saying that the Bible accounts of the creation, of the Garden of Eden, of our first parents, and of the flood are all myths, with questionable parallels in the writings of other early peoples. While orthodox Jews still believe in the Torah and what it says about Adam and Eve, even they are becoming relatively fewer in number as disbelief invades the ranks of the "chosen race."

Dictionaries also tend to deflate the Garden of Eden story and speak of Adam as simply a symbol of the "unregenerate nature of man." Adam's wife is described as merely a symbol, "an effortless feminine creature whose personal career never interferes with her role as a charming eternal Eve."

Apparently the lexicographers, like many clergymen, are not at all sure that Adam and Eve were ever real individuals who once lived and breathed here on earth, or that the Garden of Eden was anything more than the figment of someone's imagination.

A recent edition of the *Jewish Book of Knowledge* classes the stories in the five books of Moses as inventions of the Israelites, and attempts to show that similar "myths" are found in the writings of other ancient peoples. Some scholars even say the Israelites borrowed these "legends" from their neighbors. They do not take into consideration the fact that the original truthful accounts far more likely were distorted and disseminated to various parts of the earth as the Lord scattered the people when he confounded their language at Babel. It seems easier for these writers to class all accounts as legends and leave them at that.

The long-standing Christian churches for the most part accept Adam and Eve as real persons, but they so complicate their sectarian theology with peculiar concepts of the original sin and what it did to us that the average person is left actually questioning the wisdom of God and wondering whether the Deity really knew what he was about.

The Question Box, published by the Paulist Press and bearing the imprimatur of Patrick Cardinal Hayes, archbishop of New York, says that "Adam's sin was a sin of pride. . . . The eating of an apple was a trivial thing in itself, but God made it a supreme test of loyalty. It was a grievous sin, because Adam could easily have avoided it, as there was in him neither ignorance nor concupiscence, and he certainly knew, as head of the race, what terrible consequences would follow for all mankind." (Reverend Bertrand L. Conway, *The Question Box,* New York: Paulist Press, 1929, p. 219.)

The same book also calls Adam's sin "an offence of . . . prevarication," and adds, "Original Sin is indeed a great mystery, which human reason cannot fathom." (Ibid., p. 220.)

Commenting on the extreme to which some denominations had carried their belief about original sin, President Joseph Fielding Smith at one time wrote:

"When the Gospel was restored . . . there was a most pernicious doctrine being taught among the people. We may *all* be grateful to the Lord that it has almost disappeared, for it could not live in the light of the revealed Gospel. This was the doctrine that unbaptized (unsprinkled) infants, many of them not more than 'a span long,' were in hell in everlasting torment, because their parents did not have them christened by an unauthorized priest who held no divine authority. When I was in the mission field . . ., a man and his wife, unto whom I was teaching the Gospel, asked me if there was any hope for babies who die without being christened by a priest. Then they related the following story: One of their children died in early infancy. They asked the minister of their church to take charge of the funeral and give the child 'Christian burial.' This he refused to do, because, he explained, the child had not been 'baptized' and therefore could not receive Christian burial. The parents were heart-broken; they had been made to believe that their child was eternally damned, and that they need not think they would ever see it again for it was assigned to stay in the torment of hell forever. Can you imagine anything more unchristian than a teaching of this kind?" (*The Way to Perfection,* Salt Lake City: Genealogical Society of Utah, 1949, p. 198.)

The fall of Adam and Eve was no tragedy. It was a blessing in disguise, for without it none of us would have been born, since Adam and Eve, in their original state, were not able to have children, as the Book of Mormon explains:

"And now, behold, if Adam had not transgressed he would not have fallen, but he would have remained in the garden of Eden. And all things which were created must have remained in the same state in which they were after they were created; and they must have remained forever, and had no end.

"And they would have had no children; wherefore they would have remained in a state of innocence, having no joy, for they knew no misery; doing no good, for they knew no sin." (2 Nephi 2:22-23.)

Dr. James E. Talmage explained that when the temptation came in the Garden of Eden, "the woman was captivated by these representations; and, being eager to possess the advantages pictured by Satan, she disobeyed the command of the Lord, and partook of the fruit forbidden. She feared no evil *for she knew it not.* Then, telling Adam what she had done, she urged him to eat of the fruit also.

"Adam found himself in a position that made it impossible for him to obey both of the specific commandments given by the Lord. He and his wife had been commanded to multiply and replenish the earth. Adam had not yet fallen to the state of mortality, but Eve already had; and in such dissimilar conditions the two could not remain together, and therefore could not fulfil the divine requirement as to procreation. On the other hand, Adam would be disobeying another commandment by yielding to Eve's request. He deliberately and wisely decided to stand by the first and greater commandment; and, therefore, with understanding of the nature of his act, he also partook of the fruit that grew on the tree of knowledge. . . . The prophet Lehi, in expounding the scriptures to his sons, declared:

'Adam fell that man might be; and men are, that they might have joy.'"

Dr. Talmage then says:

"It has become a common practice with mankind to heap reproaches upon the progenitors of the family, and to picture the supposedly blessed state in which we would be living but for the fall; whereas our first parents are entitled to our deepest gratitude for their legacy to posterity—the means of winning glory, exaltation, and eternal lives. . . . From Father Adam we have inherited all the ills to which flesh is heir; but such are necessarily incident to a knowledge of good and evil, by the proper use of which knowledge man may become even as the Gods." (*Articles of Faith*, pp. 65, 70.)

Adam and Eve were real persons. They were the children of God. They did the will of God and opened the way for us to do likewise.

There is much significance in the genealogy of the Savior as it appears in Luke. It concludes with a listing of the generations as follows:

"Which was the son of Methusala, which was the son of Enoch, which was the son of Jared, which was the son of Maleleel, which was the son of Canaan, which was the son of Enos, which was the son of Seth, which was the son of Adam, *which was the son of God.*" (Luke 3:37-38. Italics added.)

The marriage of Adam and Eve was a reality and God performed it. President Joseph Fielding Smith is quoted as follows on this subject:

"Paul declared that, 'Neither is the man without the woman, neither the woman without the man, in the Lord.' And the Lord said he would give the man a companion who would be a help *meet* for him: that is, *a help who would answer all the requirements, not only of companionship, but also through whom the fulness of the purposes of the Lord could be accomplished regarding the mission of man through mortal life and into eternity.*

"Neither the man nor the woman [was] capable of

filling the measure of their creation alone. The union of the two was required to complete man in the image of God. The Lord said, 'Let us make man in our image, after our likeness. . . . So God created man in his own image, in the image of God created he him; male and female created he them.' (Gen. 1:26-27.)

"Moreover when the woman was presented to the man, Adam said: 'This [woman] is now bone of my bones, and flesh of my flesh.' (Gen. 2:23; Moses 3:23.) From this we understand that his union with Eve was to be everlasting. The Savior confirmed this doctrine when he said to the Jews: 'For this cause shall a man leave father and mother, and shall cleave to his wife; and *they twain shall be one flesh. Wherefore they are no more twain, but one flesh.*' (Matt. 19:5-6.) . . .

"The Prophet Joseph taught that 'marriage was *an institution of heaven,* instituted in the Garden of Eden; [and] that it is necessary it should be solemnized by the authority of the everlasting priesthood.'

"Marriage as established in the beginning was an eternal covenant. The first man and the first woman were not married until death should part them, for at that time death had not come into the world. The ceremony on that occasion was performed by the Eternal Father himself whose work endures forever. It is the will of the Lord that all marriages should be of like character, and in becoming 'one flesh' the man and the woman are to continue in the married status, according to the Lord's plan, throughout all eternity as well as in this mortal life." (Bruce R. McConkie, compiler, *Doctrines of Salvation,* Bookcraft, 1955, 2:70-71.)

Chapter Two

MICHAEL THE ARCHANGEL

Adam and Eve were the same kind of people we are. They looked like we do; they acted much as we do. They planted crops, as we do, and they ate the harvest of their fields. They had their flocks and herds, as we do, and lived a mortal existence like ours.

Adam and Eve had a preexistence, as we did. They lived before this earth was made. But in that preexistent life, who was Adam? Had he really achieved the rank of Deity, which some dissidents believe?

There is no scripture anywhere that indicates that Adam had done so, but there is abundant scripture that points to the contrary. He was an angel—a preexistent spirit like all the rest of us—except that he had reached high distinction, a place of importance and prestige; but he was an angel nevertheless.

However, Adam was an archangel. The scripture refers to him as *the* archangel. The definition of that prefix—*arch*—is chief, or preeminent. An added definition says: "most fully embodying the qualities of his kind."

Adam, then, was the chief angel, but not Deity. He embodied most fully the qualities of an angelic existence. He was preeminent among the angels. He was their leader, and his name at that time was Michael. But, we repeat, he was an *angel*.

The Prophet Joseph, speaking of the angels, said, "These angels are under the direction of Michael or Adam, who acts under the direction of the Lord."

7

(Teachings of the Prophet Joseph Smith, p. 168.)

On this same point, the Prophet also said: "The Father called all spirits before Him at the creation of man, and organized them. He (Adam) is the head, and was told to multiply." *(Teachings,* p. 158.)

In speaking of the priesthood, the Prophet said: "Christ is the Great High Priest; Adam next." *(Teachings,* p. 158.)

He referred also to the priesthood which is "after the order of the Son of God," later called the Melchizedek Priesthood to avoid the too-frequent use of the name of Deity. *(Teachings,* p. 167.)

Said the Prophet: "The Priesthood was first given to Adam; he obtained the First Presidency, and held the keys of it from generation to generation. He obtained it in the Creation, before the world was formed. . . . He had dominion given him over every living creature. He is Michael the Archangel, spoken of in the Scriptures. Then to Noah, who is Gabriel; he stands next in authority to Adam in the Priesthood; he was called of God to this office, and was the father of all living this day, and to him was given the dominion." *(Teachings,* p. 157.)

Another indication of the fact that Adam was *the* archangel, the leader of all the spirits in the pre-earth life—but always subservient to Jehovah, who was Christ—is that it was he, Michael, who led the armies of heaven in ejecting the rebellious Lucifer from the heavens when he chose to fight against God. Lucifer, it will be remembered, was also an "angel of God who was in authority in the presence of God." But he "rebelled against the Only Begotten Son whom the Father loved and who was in the bosom of the Father." (D&C 76:25.)

President Joseph Fielding Smith said this:

"In regard to the holding of the priesthood in pre-existence, I will say that there was an organization there just as well as an organization here, and men there held authority. *Men chosen to positions of trust in the spirit world held priesthood.* (Alma 13:3-9.)

"To Adam, after he was driven from the Garden of Eden, the plan of salvation was revealed, and upon him the *fullness* of the priesthood was conferred. As Michael, the prince, *he holds the keys of all dispensations,* which appointment he received under Jesus Christ, 'Who hath appointed Michael your prince, and established his feet, and set him upon high, and given unto him the *keys of salvation* under the counsel and direction of the Holy One, who is without beginning of days or end of life.' (See D&C 78:16.)

"Adam received the holy priesthood and was commanded by the Lord to teach his children the principles of the gospel. Moreover, Adam was baptized for the remission of his sins, for the same principles by which men are saved now were the principles by which men were saved in the beginning. In that day as many as repented and were baptized received the gift of the Holy Ghost by the laying on of hands. Adam made all these things known to his sons and daughters." (*Doctrines of Salvation,* Bookcraft, 1956, 3:81-82.)

Note here that Lucifer, like Michael, was an angel of God "who was in authority in the presence of God" before his rebellion. To this extent, Lucifer and Michael were similar, except that although Lucifer was an angel in great authority in the presence of God, it was Michael who was the *chief* or the *arch* angel, and not Lucifer.

Obviously they were both great spirits in that pre-earth life, both holding high authority there. But Lucifer turned traitor and allowed his ambition to blind him. Therefore he fought against God, and "was thrust down from the presence of God and the Son, and was called Perdition, for the heavens wept over him—he was Lucifer, a son of the morning." (D&C 76:25-26.)

"And there was war in heaven: Michael and his angels fought against the dragon, and the dragon

[Lucifer] fought and his angels,

"And prevailed not; neither was their place found any more in heaven.

"And the great dragon was cast out, that old serpent, called the Devil, and Satan, which deceiveth the whole world: he was cast out into the earth, and his angels were cast out with him." (Revelation 12:7-9.)

So Michael, the general of the Lord's hosts, was triumphant. But keep in mind, he was an angel even as Lucifer had been, except that Michael was righteous and loyal to Jehovah. Nevertheless, he was an angel, *the* archangel. People who attempt to credit him with divinity simply do not know the scriptures.

In his capacity of archangel, Michael even yet has a great ministry related to the latter days. He will be a key figure in announcing the time for the dead to be resurrected. ". . . before the earth shall pass away, Michael, mine archangel [note that he will still be an archangel then], shall sound his trump, and then shall all the dead awake, for their graves shall be opened, and they shall come forth—yea, even all." (D&C 29:26.)

Another great war will take place as part of the "winding-up scene." Says the scripture:

". . . Satan shall be bound, that old serpent, who is called the devil, and shall not be loosed for the space of a thousand years.

"And then he shall be loosed for a little season, that he may gather together his armies.

"And Michael, *the seventh angel, even the archangel,* shall gather together his armies, even the hosts of heaven.

"And the devil shall gather together his armies, even the hosts of hell, and shall come up to battle against Michael and his armies.

"And then cometh the battle of the great God; and the devil and his armies shall be cast away into their own place, that they shall not have power over the saints any more at all.

"For Michael shall fight their battles, and shall overcome him who seeketh the throne of him who sitteth upon the throne, even the Lamb." (D&C 88:110-115. Italics added.)

To make even more clear the fact that Michael, as an angel, works under the direction of the Savior, Jesus Christ, who is Deity and who presides over Michael, or Adam, we have this: " . . . The Lord God, . . . Who hath appointed Michael your prince, and established his feet, and set him upon high, and given unto him the keys of salvation *under the counsel and direction of the Holy One* who is without beginning of days or end of life." (D&C 78:15-16. Italics added.)

Notice the distinction between Michael and the Holy One.

The Prophet Joseph also makes it clear that not only was Adam the archangel Michael, but that he was also the same being who is mentioned in the scripture as the Ancient of Days.

When Joseph and Sidney Rigdon visited Spring Hill, Missouri, the Prophet explained that "by the mouth of the Lord it was named Adam-ondi-Ahman, because, said He, it is the place where Adam shall come to visit his people, or the Ancient of Days shall sit, as spoken of by Daniel the Prophet."(Teachings, p. 122.)

The Prophet said further on this point: "Daniel in his seventh chapter speaks of the Ancient of Days; he means the oldest man, our Father Adam, Michael, he will call his children together and hold a council with them to prepare them for the coming of the Son of Man. He (Adam) is the father of the human family, and presides over the spirits of all men, and all that have had the keys must stand before him in this grand council. This may take place before some of us leave this stage of action. The Son of Man stands before him, and there is given him glory and dominion. Adam delivers up his stewardship to Christ, that which was delivered to him as holding the keys of the universe, but retains his

11

standing as the head of the human family." (*Teachings*, p. 157.)

Then the Prophet speaks of a vision to him: "I saw Adam in the valley of Adam-ondi-Ahman. He called together his children and blessed them with a patriarchal blessing. The Lord appeared in their midst, and he (Adam) blessed them all, and foretold what should befall them to the latest generation." (*Teachings*, p. 158.)

This evidently refers to a gathering of Adam's family that was held while he himself was still in mortality. In a revelation given to the Prophet Joseph in August 1830, the Lord identified Adam as Michael in these words: "And also with Michael, or Adam, the father of all, the prince of all, the ancient of days." (D&C 27:11.)

The same identification is given in section 107, as follows: "And the Lord appeared unto them, and they rose up and blessed Adam, and called him Michael, the prince, the archangel." (D&C 107:54.)

Can anyone in reason doubt the true identity of Adam or Michael as it is set forth in these scriptures and teachings of the Prophet? To suppose that he was either God the Eternal Father or the Savior, as some dissidents teach, is obviously preposterous.

Chapter Three

ADAM WAS NOT DEITY

Adam was not Deity. He was the principal servant of Deity, being the archangel, the leader of the Lord's hosts, the general of the armies of heaven, and the first man. But he was not Deity.

Luke says he was the son of Deity, which is correct. (Luke 3:38.) President Brigham Young says that Adam was so close in his association with Deity that he was allowed to assist in the creation of the earth. But, as President Young also said, he nevertheless was Michael the archangel, and not Deity.

In discussing this, President Joseph Fielding Smith said: ". . . President Brigham Young definitely declares that Adam is Michael, the Archangel, the Ancient of Days, which indicates definitely that Adam is *not* Elohim, or the God whom we worship, who is the Father of Jesus Christ.

"Further, . . . President Young declared that Adam *helped* to make the earth. If he helped then he was *subordinate* to someone who was superior. In another paragraph in that same discourse, President Young said: 'It is true that *the earth was organized by three distinct characters,* namely, *Elohim, Jehovah,* and *Michael.*' Here he places Adam, or Michael, third in the list, and hence the least important of the three mentioned, and this President Young understood perfectly. We believe that Adam, known as Michael, had authority in the heavens before the world was framed. *He dwelt in the presence of the Father and the Son and was subject to*

13

their direction as the scriptures plainly indicate." (*Doctrines of Salvation,* Bookcraft, 1954, 1:96-97.)

Some dissidents would have us believe that Adam is our God and that we have nothing to do with any other God, which, on the face of it, is ridiculous. To say that Adam is God is, of course, opposed utterly and completely to the scriptures as well as to our Articles of Faith, in which we say: "We believe in God, the Eternal Father [meaning Elohim], and in His Son, Jesus Christ [meaning Jehovah], and in the Holy Ghost."

Adam is not so much as mentioned in that statement on the Godhead, not even by his primeval name Michael.

And to say that we have nothing to do with "any God but Adam," who is *not* a God but is the archangel, violates all the teachings of the gospel of Christ, who taught us to pray to the Father in the name of Christ, who himself provided for us all the gospel teachings, and on whose redemption we depend wholly and completely for eternal salvation, for there is none other name, under heaven, given among men whereby we may be saved. (See Acts 4:12.)

There is no such involvement with Adam, who gave us only mortality but not immortality, nor salvation, nor exaltation. These blessings come to us only through Jesus Christ the Lord.

As Peter told the people on the day of Pentecost: "Therefore let all the house of Israel know assuredly, that God hath made that same Jesus, whom ye have crucified, both Lord and Christ." (Acts 2:36.) But not so with Adam.

At this point we might paraphrase the words of Paul to the Corinthians: "Is Christ divided? Was Adam crucified for you? Or were ye baptized in the name of Adam?" (1 Corinthians 1:13.)

Don't we have everything to do with God our Eternal Father and with Jesus Christ our Savior? And the Holy Ghost—he is given to us as a companion, teacher, and revelator. That is why we as Church members have the gift of the Holy Ghost. To say we have nothing to do with the Trinity is contrary to all holy writ.

It is interesting to recall that the Book of Mormon says that Christ, not Adam, is the God of this land, even though Adam lived in what is now Missouri, USA. (See Ether 2:12.)

It is most appropriate here to quote President Joseph Fielding Smith in his classic statement: "If I ever say anything contrary to the scriptures, the scriptures prevail." This applies to all, even to Brigham Young.

In identifying Adam, President Young said: "The Lord sent forth his Gospel to the people; he said, I will give it to *my son Adam,* from whom Methuselah received it; and Noah received from Methuselah; and Melchizedek administered to Abraham." (*Discourses of Brigham Young,* Deseret Book, 1946, p. 105. Italics added.)

In a discourse in the Salt Lake Tabernacle on April 17, 1870, President Young said this: "The world may in vain ask the question: 'Who are we?' But the Gospel tells us that we are the sons and daughters of that God whom we serve. Some say, 'We are the children of Adam and Eve.' So we are, and *they* are the children of. our Heavenly Father." (*Journal of Discourses* [JD], 13:311.)

In remarks also in Salt Lake City on July 8, 1863, President Young said: "We believe in God the Father and in Jesus Christ our elder brother. We believe that God is a person of tabernacle, possessing in an infinitely higher degree all the perfections and qualifications of his mortal children. We believe that he made Adam after his own image and likeness, as Moses testified. . . ." (JD, 10:230-31.)

At another time President Young said: "Adam was as conversant with his Father who placed him upon the earth as we are conversant with our earthly parents.

The Father frequently came to visit his son Adam, and talked and walked with him; and the children of Adam were more or less acquainted with him. . . ." (JD, 9:148.)

On April 9, 1852, President Young said: "It is true that the earth was organized by three distinct characters, namely Elohim, Yahovah, and Michael, these three forming a quorum. . . ." (JD, 1:50.) Then could Adam possibly be Elohim, as some say? These were three distinct persons.

On November 6, 1864, President Young said: "Three years previous to the death of Adam, he called Seth, Enos, Cainan, Mahalaleel, Jared, Enoch, and Methuselah, who were all High Priests, with the residue of his posterity who were righteous, into the valley of Adam-ondi-Ahman, and there bestowed upon them his last blessing. And the Lord appeared unto them, and they rose up and blessed Adam, and *called him Michael, the Prince, the Archangel.*" (JD, 10:355.)

Can anyone misunderstand that plain language?

Elder Charles C. Rich, of the Council of the Twelve, was present on a day when President Young gave an address that was wrongly reported as saying Adam was Deity. In the copy of the *Journal of Discourses* that he had, Elder Rich referred to the misquotation as it appears in the *Journal of Discourses*, and in his own hand he wrote the following as the correct statement made by President Young: "Jesus our elder Brother, was begotten in the flesh by the same character who talked with Adam in the Garden of Eden, and who is our Heavenly Father." (This signed statement is in the hands of the Church Historian.)

Some of the reporters at the Tabernacle in those days were not as skilled as others, and admittedly made mistakes, such as the misquotation of President Young as above, which was corrected by Brother Rich and which has caused some persons in the Church to go astray. The erroneously reported statement had been mistakenly made to read: "Jesus, our elder brother, was begotten in the flesh by the same character that was in the garden of Eden, and who is our Father in Heaven." (JD, 1:51.)

On the face of it the mistake is obvious and was quickly noted by Elder Rich, who was present and heard the sermon. Hence the correction that he made.

That other errors were made by reporters who recorded sermons of the brethren of that day is well attested. As one case in point, we provide the following statement made on October 7, 1903, by President Joseph F. Smith:

"I want to call your attention to an important matter. There is being printed in circular form now by unauthorized persons a sermon delivered years ago by President Brigham Young on the question of High Priests and Seventies, that is not correct. When I was presiding over the British Mission some years ago, this sermon was printed in the Deseret News and when it came to Liverpool, Charles W. Nibley and Henry W. Naisbitt were laboring with me there assisting me in publishing the Millennial Star. They had the form set up ready to print and brought me the copy and I said, 'That discourse cannot be printed in the Star.' 'But,' said Brother Nibley, 'is it not the sermon of President Brigham Young?' 'Perhaps it is,' said I, 'but it can not go in the Star.' Then these brethren took up a labor with me to convince me that I had no business to interfere with President's discourses. I said, 'It makes no difference, that discourse is not true as it is before you, it does not state the truth, it is not true, it is contrary to the word of the Lord and it can not be put in the Star.' Next morning I heard a rap at the door and when I asked what was the matter, this was long before daylight, and when I went to see, lo and behold it was a cablegram from President Brigham Young, commanding me not to publish that discourse in the Millennial Star, and it never was printed, by the authority of President Brigham

Young." (Quoted in Daily Journal of John M. Whitaker, p. 95, in files of Church Historical Department.)

"Note: The Millennial Star was first published by Joseph F. Smith on Monday, June 4, 1877 - Albert Carrington, in his last issue quoted from the May 1 issue of the Deseret News. *From April 1 to the demise of President Brigham Young, there were in the Deseret News eight discourses of Brigham Young that were not printed in the Millennial Star:*

1. p. 225 - May 6th 1877
2. p. 247 - April 6th 1877
3. p. 274 - May 25th 1877
4. p. 306 - May 18 1877
5. p. 358 - April 29th 1877
6. p. 418 - July 24, 1877
7. p. 434 - June 17th 1877
8. p. 482 - August 19, 1877"

(John M. Whitaker Journal, vol. 2, p. 566.)

This latter note itself is very significant. There was evidently good reason for these discourses not being published.

During the Reed Smoot investigation, President Charles W. Penrose was quizzed concerning the reliability of the *Journal of Discourses*, and he too admitted mistakes had been made by reporters, asserting that some of those volumes contain sermons "the authenticity of which has been disputed."

As taken from the official record, his testimony reads as follows. The lawyer questioning him was Robert W. Tayler.

"Mr. Tayler. There were publications known as the 'Journal of Discourses?'

"Mr. Penrose. Yes.

"Mr. Tayler. They were published by the church?

"Mr. Penrose. I think they were published by George D. Watt and J.D. Long, originally, in Liverpool, England.

"Mr. Tayler. In the interest of the church?

"Mr. Penrose. Of course they were all supposed to be in the interest of the Church, but I don't think the Church published them. I am not sure about that.

"Mr. Tayler. Have you ever heard the authority of that publication questioned? . . .

"Mr. Penrose. In what way do you mean? . . .

"Mr. Tayler. Can you answer the question—the correctness of the publication?

"Mr. Penrose. Do you mean the correctness of its contents?

"Mr. Tayler. Yes.

"Mr. Penrose. Oh yes, there are some things in there that have been disputed.

"Mr. Tayler. That is, disputed by the persons who spoke them?

"Mr. Penrose. Oh, no; disputed by others. . . . *We did not regard these books as authorities, only as works of reference*, sometimes, to give the ideas that these men maintained on these subjects. . . . I may add to that, Mr. Tayler, if you will allow me, that there are some sermons published in the Journal of Discourses the authenticity of which has been disputed—for instance, some of the sermons attributed to Joseph Smith, the prophet. They were taken down at the time in long-hand and have been published in the Journal of Discourses and there have been disputes as to their correctness." (Reed Smoot Investigation, vol. 2, Dec. 20, 1904, pp. 440-42. Italics added.)

President John Taylor was a close associate of the Prophet Joseph Smith and learned doctrine from him. He also was close to President Brigham Young in the ministry. Following are some quotations from sermons of President Taylor as provided in *The Gospel Kingdom*, a compilation of his work used as a textbook a few years ago in the priesthood quorums of the Church. (Bookcraft, 1964. Italics added.)

On page 91 of that book we read: "How did Adam

get his information of the things of God? He got it through the gospel of Jesus Christ, and through this same priesthood of which we have been speaking. *God came to him in the Garden and talked with him.*" This supports the correction by Charles C. Rich to which we have previously referred.

On page 96 we find this: "Adam and Eve both considered that they had gained, instead of suffered loss, through their disobedience to that law. . . . By pursuing the course they did, through the atonement, *they would see God as they had done before.*"

On page 97: "When Adam and Eve ate of the forbidden fruit, the mercy of God was extended to them, and they perceived as Eve expressed it, that if there had been no fall, they would have had no posterity. . . ." Page 98: "And so Adam and Eve rejoiced in their hearts that God had provided the plan, and although they were fallen, yet in this life, through the atonement, they would have joy, and by and by they would *return to their Father*, and there rejoice exceedingly in the abundant mercy of God, and in the redemption wrought out for them by the Son of God."

It is plain to see here that President Taylor had no thought of Adam being God. Otherwise his remarks would not make sense. But they do reflect the correct teachings of the Prophet Joseph Smith.

On page 102, President Taylor is quoted pertaining to the land of Adam-ondi-Ahman, "or in other words, the valley where God talked with Adam."

On page 218 of this same book we read from President Taylor: "When Adam was driven from the garden, an angel was placed with a flaming sword to guard the way of the tree of life, lest man should eat of it and become immortal in his degenerate state, and thus be incapable of obtaining that exaltation which he would be capable of enjoying through the redemption of Jesus Christ, and the power of the resurrection, with his renewed and glorified body. Having tasted of the nature of the fall, and having grappled with sin and misery, knowing, *like the Gods,* both good and evil, having, like Jesus, overcome the evil, and through the power of the atonement having conquered death, hell, and the grave, he regains that paradise from which he was banished, not in the capacity of ignorant man, unacquainted with evil, *but like unto a God.*"

This is interesting—Adam, being saved through the atonement of the Savior, could become "like unto a God," which is true likewise of the rest of us who obey the gospel. He had come to know good and evil through the fall, and thus in this respect became "like the Gods," said President Taylor. But at no time does President Taylor say that Adam *was* God, for he was then and still is the archangel.

The scriptures are interesting on this point.

The King James Bible, speaking of the temptation, quotes the devil as saying to Eve: "... your eyes shall be opened, and ye shall be as the gods, knowing good and evil." (Genesis 3:5.)

And after the fall we read: "And the Lord God said, Behold, the man is become *as one of us,* to know good and evil...." (Genesis 3:22. Italics added.)

The Knox Catholic Bible reads: "He [the Lord] said, Here is Adam become *like one of ourselves,* with knowledge of good and evil."

The Moffatt version says: "Then said God the Eternal, man has become *like one of us,* he knows good and evil."

The Goodspeed Bible reads: "Then the Lord God said, See the man has become *like one of us,* in knowing good from evil."

The Pearl of Great Price says: "And I, the Lord God, said unto mine Only Begotten: Behold, *the man is become as one of us* to know good and evil...." (Moses 4:28. Italics added.)

The latter version is most interesting and should refute any and all claims that Adam was the Father of

21

Jesus Christ, or that he was Deity at all, for "the man" spoken of was Adam, fully separate and apart from the Father and the Son.

Note that the Almighty was with the Savior and spoke to him about Adam—a *third party*. He referred to Adam as the man—this third party—who now had achieved a likeness to the Father and the Son in that he now knew the difference between good and evil.

Any fair-minded person capable of reading ordinary English should recognize that Adam was a third party in this situation. The Father and the Son spoke to each other *about* this third party. Adam was not a party to the conversation. He was now a mortal being as a result of the fall, and he had just learned the difference between good and evil. The Eternal Father and the Son, Jehovah, already knew this difference from some previous unrecorded experience. It was Adam's first experience, his great discovery. And in this sense, what Satan said became a fact—he had become as the Gods, knowing good and evil. All of these scriptures show the separateness between Adam and the Deity.

When the Father spoke of his Beloved Son and said, "I, the Lord God, said unto mine Only Begotten: Behold, the man is become as one of us," he was in no manner referring to himself as being Adam, nor did he indicate that Adam was the Father. The whole mistaken Adam-God concept becomes a ridiculous contradiction in the light of this one single scripture.

President Wilford Woodruff, who was also taught by both the Prophet Joseph and Brigham Young and was a close associate of President Taylor, certainly knew the correct identity of Adam. In his journal of January 21, 1867, he wrote: "Who was Michael, the Archangel?" "He is Adam. . . ." (Matthias F. Cowley, *Wilford Woodruff*, Deseret News, 1909, p. 450.)

President Joseph Fielding Smith wrote in a letter:

"President Brigham Young was thoroughly acquainted with the doctrine of the Church. He studied the Doctrine and Covenants and many times quoted from it, the particular passages concerning the relationship of Adam to Jesus Christ. He knew perfectly well that Adam had been placed at the head of the human family by commandment of the Father, and this doctrine he taught during the many years of his ministry."

President Smith also wrote: "This doctrine was taught by Joseph Smith, who said:

" 'The Priesthood was first given to Adam. He obtained it in the Creation, before the world was formed. He had dominion given him over every living creature. He is Michael the Archangel, spoken of in the scriptures. . . . The Priesthood is an everlasting principle, and existed with God from eternity, and will to eternity, without beginning of days or end of years. The keys have to be brought from heaven whenever the gospel is sent. When they are revealed from heaven, it is by Adam's authority. . . . Christ is the Great High Priest, Adam next.'

"If the keys of salvation have been committed to the hands of Adam, under the direction of Jesus Christ, then is there anything out of place for President Brigham Young to declare that it is Adam with whom we have to do? And yet here is the acknowledgment of the superiority of Jesus Christ. This being true, then the human family is immediately subject to Adam and he to the Redeemer of the world. Again, to illustrate this point:

"In the Church we have a presiding officer whom we call the bishop; he has full charge in the ward over which he presides. This bishop is subject to the direction of the stake president, and he in turn to the Presidency of the Church. The only one, in the same sense, with whom the members have to do is the bishop, but he is not the superior officer by any means.

"In another revelation which President Young taught many times, we find the following:

" 'Wherefore, verily I say unto you that all things

unto me are spiritual, and not at any time have I given you a law which was temporal; neither any men, nor the children of men; *neither Adam, your father, whom I created.*' [D&C 29:34. Italics added.]

"The doctrine taught by the Church in relation to Adam is clearly defined in the following taken from the 107th Section of the Doctrine and Covenants.

" 'Three years previous to the death of Adam, he called Seth, Enos, Cainan, Mahalaleel, Jared, Enoch, and Methuselah, who were all high priests, with the residue of his posterity who were righteous, into the valley of Adam-ondi-Ahman, and there bestowed upon them his last blessing.

" 'And the Lord appeared unto them, and they rose up and blessed Adam, and called him Michael, the prince, the archangel.

" 'And the Lord administered comfort unto Adam, and said unto him: I have set thee to be at the head; a multitude of nations shall come of thee, and thou art a prince over them forever.

" 'And Adam stood up in the midst of the congregation; and, notwithstanding he was bowed down with age, being full of the Holy Ghost, predicted whatever should befall his posterity unto the latest generation.' [D&C 107:53-56.]

"From these passages President Brigham Young could very properly say that we are subject to Adam; that he rules over his posterity, and he gives us commandment, even as he receives commandment from Jesus Christ who directs him in his ministry and will do so to the latest day of time. And this does not detract anything from the power, greatness and glory of God the Father and His Son Jesus Christ." (Personal correspondence.)

Chapter Four

IS IT ALL
A MYTH?

Is the story of Adam and Eve and the Garden of Eden and the fall all a myth, as atheists and higher critics claim?

What is a myth?

One of Webster's definitions reads: "a story invented as a veiled explanation of a truth." The dictionary also defines a myth as "a story that is usually of unknown origin and at least partially traditional, that ostensibly relates historical events usually of such character as to serve to explain some practice, belief, institution, or natural phenomenon, and that especially associated with religious rites and beliefs." Then it gives as synonyms: "legends, allegories, and sagas."

Those who say that the story of Adam and Eve is but a legend or myth must, of course, thereby declare it to be untrue. Hence they must brand as unreliable the source of the story, and its teller as a fabricator.

Likewise, all who relate the account of Adam and Eve as though it were true must be discredited then as persons perpetuating an untruth.

Does any Latter-day Saint who has any faith at all in God wish to class the story of Adam and Eve, and the account of their fall and subsequent dealings with God, as a falsehood? Is it an unfounded legend, the figment of someone's imagination?

We might well remember that it is the Bible that tells this story, and we believe the Bible to be the word of God.

The Book of Mormon sustains the same story and adds thereto. We believe it to be the word of God too.

The Pearl of Great Price goes into great detail concerning Adam, his creation, the fall, his subsequent dealings with God, his baptism, and his covenants with God. It relates that Adam lived and taught his family the truth about the gospel. We also believe the Pearl of Great Price to be the word of God. It tells the truth.

The Doctrine and Covenants is filled with references to Adam, the fall, the redemption from that fall, the bestowing of the priesthood, and the manner in which that priesthood was handed down from one generation to another. It goes to great lengths in affirming the atonement of Christ, who did indeed redeem us from the fall of Adam. That is no myth!

We most sincerely declare the Doctrine and Covenants to be the word of God. It tells the very truth about Adam and is divinely given.

The Prophet Joseph Smith spoke often concerning Adam and his mission. Likewise have all of the subsequent presidents of the Church whom we sustain as inspired prophets, seers, and revelators—men of truth, men of God, men of revelation. Did they teach myths? Did they mislead the people? Of course not. We have the testimony that what they taught was the word of God. The Almighty himself said so in these direct words:

" . . . they shall speak as they are moved upon by the Holy Ghost.

"And whatsoever they shall speak when moved upon by the Holy Ghost shall be scripture, shall be the will of the Lord, shall be the mind of the Lord, shall be the voice of the Lord, and the power of God unto salvation." (D&C 68:3-4.)

It is essential to say that the account of Adam, his fall, and his subsequent ministry is one of the basic foundation stones of our religion. It is vital and true. Without it we would have no gospel of Christ.

If we reject Adam, we must in all consistency likewise reject Christ, for it was Christ who atoned for

Adam's sin. So if we reject the fall, we must also reject the redemption. And if we reject the fall, which brought death into the world, we must also deny the resurrection from the dead. But we cannot deny the resurrection, for thereby we would deny the Savior.

We also would reject the entire restoration of the gospel, for it was brought to earth by resurrected servants of God — Moroni, John the Baptist, Peter and James, who, with John, a translated person, ministered to Joseph Smith. Hence, if we reject Adam, we must reject Joseph Smith and all he stood for and taught. What true Latter-day Saint is prepared to do that?

There are scores of references in our modern scriptures to Adam and Eve, the fall, and the redemption. Note this from the Doctrine and Covenants:

"The order of this priesthood was confirmed to be handed down from father to son, and rightly belongs to the literal descendants of the chosen seed, to whom the promises were made.

"This order was instituted in the days of Adam, and came down by lineage in the following manner:

"From Adam to Seth, who was ordained by Adam at the age of sixty-nine years, and was blessed by him three years previous to his (Adam's) death, and received the promise of God by his father, that his posterity should be the chosen of the Lord, and that they should be preserved unto the end of the earth;

"Because he (Seth) was a perfect man, and his likeness was the express likeness of his father, insomuch that he seemed to be like unto his father in all things, and could be distinguished from him only by his age.

"Enos was ordained at the age of one hundred and thiry-four years and four months, by the hand of Adam.

"God called upon Cainan in the wilderness in the fortieth year of his age; and he met Adam in journeying to the place Shedolamak. He was eighty-seven years old when he received his ordination.

"Mahalaleel was four hundred and ninety-six years

27

and seven days old when he was ordained by the hand of Adam, who also blessed him.

"Jared was two hundred years old when he was ordained under the hand of Adam, who also blessed him.

"Enoch was twenty-five years old when he was ordained under the hand of Adam; and he was sixty-five and Adam blessed him.

"And he saw the Lord, and he walked with him, and was before his face continually; and he walked with God three hundred and sixty-five years, making him four hundred and thirty years old when he was translated.

"Methuselah was one hundred years old when he was ordained under the hand of Adam.

"Lamech was thirty-two years old when he was ordained under the hand of Seth.

"Noah was ten years old when he was ordained under the hand of Methuselah.

"Three years previous to the death of Adam, he called Seth, Enos, Cainan, Mahalaleel, Jared, Enoch, and Methuselah, who were all high priests, with the residue of his posterity who were righteous, into the valley of Adam-ondi-Ahman, and there bestowed upon them his last blessing.

"And the Lord appeared unto them, and they rose up and blessed Adam, and called him Michael, the prince, the archangel.

"And the Lord administered comfort unto Adam, and said unto him: I have set thee to be at the head; a multitude of nations shall come of thee, and thou art a prince over them forever.

"And Adam stood up in the midst of the congregation; and notwithstanding he was bowed down with age, being full of the Holy Ghost, predicted whatsoever should befall his posterity unto the latest generation.

"These things were all written in the book of Enoch, and are to be testified of in due time." (D&C 107:40-57.)

And read what the Doctrine and Covenants says in section 84 as it discusses the descent of the priesthood:

"Which Abraham received the priesthood from Melchizedek, who received it through the lineage of his fathers, even till Noah;

"And from Noah till Enoch, through the lineage of their fathers;

"And from Enoch to Abel, who was slain by the conspiracy of his brother, who received the priesthood by the commandments of God, by the hand of his father Adam, *who was the first man—*

"Which priesthood continueth in the church of God in all generations, and is without beginning of days or end of years.

"And the Lord confirmed a priesthood also upon Aaron and his seed, throughout all their generations, which priesthood also continueth and abideth forever with the priesthood which is after the holiest order of God.

"And this greater priesthood administereth the gospel and holdeth the key of the mysteries of the kingdom, even the key of the knowledge of God.

"Therefore, in the ordinances thereof, the power of godliness is manifest." (D&C 84:14-20. Italics added.)

In numerous quotations from the Book of Mormon we learn that Adam indeed was a reality, a great high priest, the progenitor of all mankind in the flesh. No one reading the Book of Mormon can reasonably doubt the existence, the fall, and the mission of Adam and Eve.

As an example, ponder the following:

"And after Adam and Eve had partaken of the forbidden fruit they were driven out of the garden of Eden, to till the earth.

"And they have brought forth children; yea, even the family of all the earth.

"And the days of the children of men were prolonged, according to the will of God, that they might repent while in the flesh; wherefore, their state became a state of probation, and their time lengthened according to the commandments which the Lord God gave unto the children of men. For he gave commandment that all men must repent; for he showed unto all men that they were lost, because of the transgression of their parents.

"And now, behold, if Adam had not transgressed he would not have fallen, but he would have remained in the Garden of Eden. And all things which were created must have remained in the same state in which they were after they were created; and they must have remained forever, and had no end.

"And they would have had no children; wherefore they would have remained in a state of innocence, having no joy, for they knew no misery; doing no good, for they knew no sin.

"But behold, all things have been done in the wisdom of him who knoweth all things.

"Adam fell that men might be; and men are, that they might have joy.

"And the Messiah cometh in the fulness of time, that he may redeem the children of men from the fall. And because that they are redeemed from the fall they have become free forever, knowing good from evil; to act for themselves and not to be acted upon, save it be by the punishment of the law at the great and last day, according to the commandments which God hath given.

"Wherefore, men are free according to the flesh; and all things are given them which are expedient unto man. And they are free to choose liberty and eternal life, through the great mediation of all men, or to choose captivity and death, according to the captivity and power of the devil; for he seeketh that all men might be miserable like unto himself." (2 Nephi 2:19-27.)

The Pearl of Great Price tells details of the life of Adam and Eve, their creation, and ministry. It explains too how, before the world was made, the Christ was chosen as the Redeemer, to bring about the redemption upon which the whole plan of God is based, *and that plan included the fall of Adam.*

For man to progress, he had to become mortal. It was according to God's eternal plan. Mortality was accomplished through the fall of Adam. Hence Jesus, as Jehovah, in our preexistent state accepted the over-all plan of the Eternal Father, *including the fall,* volunteered himself as our Redeemer, and prepared even then to accomplish our redemption.

Of course Adam lived. So did his wife Eve. And of course there was a fall and a redemption. To reject all of this is to reject the entire plan of salvation and turn our backs upon the Lord.

All Bible readers love the fifteenth chapter of First Corinthians, wherein the Apostle Paul bears his testimony pertaining to both Adam and the Savior. There he affirms in all soberness the fact of the redemption. Note his words:

"Now if Christ be preached that he rose from the dead, how say some among you that there is no resurrection of the dead?

"But if there be no resurrection of the dead, then is Christ not risen:

"And if Christ be not risen, then is our preaching vain, and your faith is also vain.

"Yea, and we are found false witnesses of God; because we have testified of God that he raised up Christ: whom he raised not up, if so be that the dead rise not.

"For if the dead rise not, then is not Christ raised:

"And if Christ be not raised, your faith is vain; ye are yet in your sins.

"Then they also which are fallen asleep in Christ are perished.

"If in this life only we have hope in Christ, we are of all men most miserable.

"But now is Christ risen from the dead, and become the firstfruits of them that slept.

"For since by man came death, by man came also the resurrection of the dead.

"For as in Adam all die, even so in Christ shall all be made alive." (1 Corinthians 15:12-22.)

Chapter Five

THE BIBLE CRITICS

The Bible has withstood many an onslaught. But it remains today the best seller of all books, and has been so for years. And why? Because there is a special power about the Bible. God has preserved it. God has put into the hearts of honest men and women a reverence for the Bible. They believe it. They have fought for it over the years. Some have died for it.

Think of William Tyndale, for example. It was a spiritually blind clergy and a stubborn, equally blind monarch who put him to death. It is no wonder that as he drew his last breath in martyrdom he cried out: "Lord, open the King of England's eyes." Death came after a cruel eighteen months imprisonment, forced upon him merely because he published the word of God!

Why did he thus sacrifice himself? Because he was inspired to do so — inspired to help break the shackles of ignorance that prevailed at that time, inspired to help open the way for the restoration of the gospel by the Prophet Joseph Smith.

And consider John Wycliffe, who was buffeted about in every conceivable and cruel manner for a similar reason. He too was inspired to bring to light the word of God, in an age of utter darkness, by putting the scriptures into the hands of the common people who needed them so much. And how blind were the clerics and the rulers who sought to crush that movement! In their ignorance they tried to douse the flame of genuine

33

faith and the light of revelation found within the sacred pages of holy writ.

God knew what he was about. *He preserved the Bible,* first as it was being compiled, and then he brought it forth from darkness in preparation for the restoration of his gospel in these last days. It is the *"book of the Lamb of God."* Said Nephi concerning it:

"And the angel said unto me: Knowest thou the meaning of the book?

"And I said unto him: I know not.

"And he said: Behold it proceedeth out of the mouth of a Jew. And I, Nephi, beheld it; and he said unto me: The book that thou beholdest is a record of the Jews, which contains the covenants of the Lord, which he hath made unto the house of Israel; and it also containeth many of the prophecies of the holy prophets; and it is a record like unto the engravings which are upon the plates of brass, save there are not so many; nevertheless, they contain the covenants of the Lord, which he hath made unto the house of Israel; wherefore, they are of great worth unto the Gentiles.

"And the angel of the Lord said unto me: Thou hast beheld that the book proceeded forth from the mouth of a Jew; and when it proceeded forth from the mouth of a Jew it contained the plainness of the gospel of the Lord, of whom the twelve apostles bear record; and they bear record according to the truth which is in the Lamb of God.

"Wherefore, these things go forth from the Jews in purity unto the Gentiles, according to the truth which is in God.

"And after they go forth by the hand of the twelve apostles of the Lamb, from the Jews unto the Gentiles, thou seest the foundation of a great and abominable church, which is most abominable above all other churches; for behold, they have taken away from the gospel of the Lamb many parts which are plain and most precious; and also many covenants of the Lord have they taken away.

"And all this have they done that they might pervert the right ways of the Lord, that they might blind the eyes and harden the hearts of the children of men.

"Wherefore, thou seest that after the book hath gone forth through the hands of the great and abominable church, that there are many plain and precious things taken away from the book, *which is the book of the Lamb of God.*

"And after these plain and precious things were taken away it goeth forth unto all the nations of the Gentiles; and after it goeth forth unto all the nations of the Gentiles, yea, even across the many waters which thou hast seen with the Gentiles which have gone forth out of captivity, thou seest—because of the many plain and precious things which have been taken out of the book, which were plain unto the understanding of the children of men, according to the plainness which is in the Lamb of God—because of these things which are taken away out of the gospel of the Lamb, an exceeding great many do stumble, yea, insomuch that Satan hath great power over them." (1 Nephi 13:21-29. Italics added.)

The Bible in and of itself is a divine miracle. The preservation of the Bible and its survival to our day is likewise a miracle. The fact that it has endured the merciless onslaughts of blinded clerics, ignorant and prejudiced kings and governors, not to mention the later attacks of a misguided intelligentsia, is also a miracle. In spite of its losses as described by Nephi, it is still a pillar for God in these last days, and contains his true word "as far as it is translated correctly."

But we do not need to worry too much about those words — "as far as it is translated correctly" — for now, in a time when there are literally scores of translations, these new versions firmly declare the existence of God, the mission and atonement of the Savior, and the story of Adam and Eve, given as fact, not fiction.

35

So the Bible declares the word of God. It teaches all who will hear the truth of the gospel and specifically says that there was a fall in the Garden of Eden, and that there was and is a redemption by the Son of God, Jesus the Christ.

The Book of Mormon sustains the Bible as the word of God.

The Doctrine of Covenants sustains the Bible as the word of God.

The Prophet Joseph sustained the Bible as the word of God.

And so must we!

As Latter-day Saints we must ask ourselves whether we shall align ourselves with the critics of the Bible who denounce the story of Adam and Eve, or whether we shall accept the scriptures as fact and as the revealed word of the Lord. To the faithful, there can be but one choice. It is a case of the wisdom of man vs. the wisdom of God, and according to the Lord, the wisdom of man is foolishness to him. (1 Corinthians 3:19.)

The integrity of the Bible is without successful challenge. Like the Jewish race, it has been preserved for the purposes of the Lord, and as one writer has said: "Without the Bible it is impossible to imagine that the Jews could have survived as a distinctive people or as a religious fellowship for so many centuries and through so many vicissitudes." (Nathan Ausubel, in *The Book of Jewish Knowledge,* New York: Crown Publishers, 1964, p. 38.)

The truth of the Bible, as a whole, is a testimony also of its contents, which provide the account of Adam and Eve and the closely related subject of the atonement of the Savior.

The combined weight of evidence *for* the Bible is so much greater than the evidence against it (which is largely conjecture and hypothesis) that the opposition hardly deserves serious consideration. Especially is this true so far as Latter-day Saints are concerned, for in modern revelation the Lord himself sustains it.

Bible archaeology in recent years has opened a new door to increased faith in this sacred word. The discoveries of actual places and the confirmation of actual events related in the Bible are now coming forth in great number. The discovery of ancient libraries of historical writings alone has been extensive. These help to confirm the Bible. No one any longer need be a victim of vicious and often unscholarly criticism of holy writ.

While critics seek to discredit the Bible, the champions of this inspired volume strike back in words far more understandable and forceful. Can any of those critics be considered as great as the defenders named below?

Consider just a few of their comments:

The scripture was so important to George Washington, the first president of the United States, that he said: "It is impossible to rightly govern the world without God and the Bible."

William Gladstone said: "I have known ninety-five of the world's great men in my time, and of these, eight-seven were followers of the Bible. The Bible is stamped with a Specialty of Origin and an immeasurable distance separates it from all competitors."

Abraham Lincoln said: "I believe the Bible is the best gift God has ever given to man. All the good from the Saviour of the world is communicated to us through this book."

And Thomas Carlyle: "The Bible is the truest utterance that ever came by alphabetic letters from the soul of man, through which, as through a window divinely opened, all men can look into the stillness of eternity and discern in glimpses their far-distant, long-forgotten home."

The German philosopher Immanuel Kant said: "The existence of the Bible as a book for the people is the greatest benefit which the human race has ever experienced. Every attempt to belittle it is a crime against humanity."

John Quincy Adams, sixth president of the United States, said: "I have made it a practice for several years to read the Bible through in the course of every year. I usually devote to this reading the first hour after I rise every morning."

Horace Greeley said: "It is impossible to mentally or socially enslave a Bible-reading people."

Dwight L. Moody made this interesting comment: "I know the Bible is inspired because it inspires me."

(All of the above comments are from Emerson Roy West, *Vital Quotations*, Bookcraft, 1968, pp. 22-23.)

Chapter Six

THE
TRUE
CREATION

The story of the creation is the most vigorously condemned portion of the Bible in the minds of the intelligentsia.

Evolutionists now point to one discovery after another in an effort to bolster their claims. But the most they can do is to point to an isolated bone here and an isolated skull there, which they themselves evolve into missing links and so-called pre-men.

No one has ever found a missing link, because there is none. Never has there been any solid proof of man's descent or ascent from the lower forms of life, or even his relationship thereto. It is all conjecture. And never has there been any acceptable evidence that creation came about by accident, for this, too, is conjecture.

As Sir Ambrose Fleming, noted British scientist, said in his *Origin of Mankind:* "We have no scientific ground, then, for supposing that the vastly more complicated structure we call the physical Universe has come into existence by a process of self-creation or accident, and without any connection with or dependence on an intelligent Thinker." (London and Edinburgh: Marshall, Morgan and Scott Ltd., 1935, p. 48.)

It was Sir James Jeans, British astronomer, who wrote: "This new knowledge compels us to revise our hasty first impressions that we had stumbled into a universe which either did not concern itself with life or was actively hostile to life. . . . We discover that the universe shows evidence of a designing or controlling power that has something in common with our own individual minds." (*The Mysterious Universe,* New York: The Macmillan Co., 1930, pp. 158-59.)

Einstein said: "The harmony of natural law reveals an Intelligence of such superiority that, compared with it, all the systematic thinking and acting of human beings is an utterly insignificant reflection." (Alfred G. Fisk, *The Search for Life's Meaning,* New York: Fleming H. Revell Co., 1946, p. 90.)

Fraser-Harris, British physiologist, wrote: "So striking a oneness is perceived throughout the Universe, such a high degree of precision characterizes both nonliving and living matter that we seem forced to picture the Universe as the outcome of an Intelligent Purpose. Each of the sciences tells the same story— self-consistent uniformity of plan." (Ibid., p. 90.)

A most interesting observation on the creation comes from the man who pioneered the computer, which today has taken such an important part in our lives. Dr. Claude M. Hathaway, designer of the "electronic brain" for the National Advisory Committee on Aeronautics and a designer for the General Electric Company, wrote:

". . . *design requires a designer.* This most fundamental rational reason for my belief in God is one which has been greatly bolstered by my engineering experience. After years of work in the development and design of complicated mechanisms and electronic circuitry I have acquired a tremendous appreciation for *design* wherever I find it. With such a background, it is unthinkable that the inconceivably marvelous design in the world around us could be anything else than the product of a personal and infinitely intelligent Designer. Certainly, this is an old argument that modern science had made more powerful than ever before. . . .

"After working on this computer for a year or two, and after facing and solving the many design problems which it presented, it is completely irrational to me to think that such a device could come into being in any other way than through the agency of an intelligent designer.

"Now, the world around us is a vast assembly of design or order, independent but interrelated, vastly more complex in every small detail than my 'electronic brain.' If my computer required a designer, how much more so did that complex physio-chemical-biological machine which is my human body—which in turn is but an extremely minute part of the well nigh infinite cosmos?

"Design, order, arrangement, call it what you will, can result from only two causes: chance or design. The more complex the order, the more remote the possibility of chance. Placed as we are in the midst of design little short of infinite, I cannot help but believe in God." (John Clover Monsma, *The Evidence of God in an Expanding Universe*, New York: G.P. Putnam's Sons, 1958, pp. 144-45.)

This reminds us of a statement made by Dr. Arthur H. Compton, Nobel Prize winner, who wrote an article entitled "What You and I Need to Know" as far back as April 13, 1941. He wrote in the *Los Angeles Times* as follows: "Where there is plan, there is intelligence, and an orderly unfolding universe testifies to the truth of the most majestic statement ever uttered—in the beginning—GOD."

Dr. Henry Eyring is a great Mormon scientist who has eight doctorate degrees. He has served as president of the American Chemical Society and of the American Association for the Advancement of Science. He holds the nation's top scientific honor, the National Medal of Science, which was presented to him by President Lyndon B. Johnson. In his book *The Faith of a Scientist*, he says: "I worship the Supreme Intelligence of the universe and I am convinced that, wise as men are and in spite of the wonderful things they have done, the

Creator of this universe goes so far beyond anything that men understand that it is ridiculous to talk of the two in the same terms. So far as I have been able to observe, those who study deeply into scientific matters are often of that persuasion.

"Since all truth has a single source, the apparent conflicts [between science and religion] that often trouble us reflect only our incomplete understanding. . . ." (*The Faith of a Scientist,* Bookcraft, 1967, p. 107.)

"I believe that every brilliant conquest made by man is but a manifestation of the divine spark which sets him apart from the rest of creation. Man is in the image of God, destined to go on learning and perfecting himself throughout eternity. To accept the idea that the human personality ends with death is to accept life as a futile, meaningless gesture." (Ibid., p. 98.)

It is interesting that Dr. Eyring then quotes Dr. Harlow Shapley as saying that there are numerous planets in the heavens on which it is reasonable to suppose life could or does exist. (Harlow Shapley, *Of Stars and Man*, p. 74)

Dr. Eyring continues: "It is accordingly natural to . conclude that the universe is flooded with intelligent beings and, presumably, always has been. Any unfolding of intelligences that may eventuate on this earth only repeats what has happened previously elsewhere." (Ibid.)

Yes, God lives. He gave us our creation, our earth, and all that is in it. He gave us also the sacred story of creation. He gave us the scriptures which provide it, and he gave us the testimony, his own testimony, that it is all true.

The discoveries of the anthropologists and their interpretation of those findings seem on the surface to be very convincing, but when they are carefully examined, they still are found to rest only upon hypothesis.

Unfortunately, such views are finding their way into the textbooks of our public schools and are being presented as though they were facts, as though they were proven beyond question. Hence our children are learning to accept those theories as facts and to regard evolution as the only true explanation of the origin of life. But not all scientists agree with the anthropologists by any means. For example:

Dr. Gerald T. Den Hartog, research agronomist for the U.S. Department of Agriculture, writes: "By natural selection and human selection progress has been made in obtaining biotypes *within* each of the domesticated species. . . . However—and this is the great point to be stressed—basically the plant species remain the same all through the ages, regardless of selective processes, changes in climate and environment, or persistent and widespread attacks by biological enemies. The Creator's mandate in Genesis 1 is being carried out to this very day.

"A striking illustration of the persistency of plant species is provided by the archaeologists' finds of wheat seed and other plant products that correspond to our present-day species and that have remained relatively unchanged over thousands of years. . . .

"Plants reproduce after their kind, *unfailingly*. Inheritance does not proceed in a wild, haphazard, uncontrolled manner. Wheat produces wheat, barley barley, an olive tree an olive tree, under all sorts of environment, generation after generation.

"To me, this indicates the existence of a Creator-God, limitless both in knowledge and in power." (Monsma, *op. cit.*, pp. 103-105.)

Agreeing with him is Dr. Walter Edward Lammerts, University of California geneticist, who says that although some mutations are obtained and are eagerly pointed to by evolutionists, as a rule they do not survive. ". . . most mutations are lethal," he says. ". . . the science of genetics offeres no evidence for belief in the two most basic assumptions of Charles Darwin. . . . Except for occasional mutations (changes), such lines breed true and do not vary in all possible directions as postulated by Darwin." (Ibid., p. 114.)

Dr. Lester Zimmerman, of Purdue University, specialist in plants and soils for the U.S. Soil Conservation Service, asked the question: "Who was it that established and set in motion the laws of genetics and plant growth? . . . Where did the first plants come from? . . . a chance origin is logically out of the question, and the assumption of an intelligent originator is imperative: Who made the first plants?"

He then quotes Job, chapter 38, and concludes: "The answer of the Book of Job to the question of the origin and maintenance of the universe (and that naturally includes the plant world) is *my* answer. All Nature was originated by God, and He sustains it, incessantly." (Ibid., pp. 195-96.)

And the same reply refers to man as well as to plant life. Dr. Alfred G. Fisk of San Francisco State University, who wrote his *Search for Life's Meaning* to be used in philosophy classes at that school, quoted numerous outstanding scientists indicating that they believed in a divine creation by an Intelligent Designer. He then said: "Similar quotations from any number of leading scientists could be added to these we have given— including such names as those of the Nobel Prize winners, Compton and Millikan; the professor of geology at Harvard University, Kirtley F. Mather, and the great physicist, Michael Pupin. These scientists are not speaking from the point of view of religious experience; they are interpreting the world opened up to view by the scientific inquiry. It is in their judgment a world of unified structure, of order, of design. This unity implies to them, as it does to us, an Organizer, Designer, Orderer. Understanding the 'laws' of chance, these scientists know that it is not reasonable to suppose that the orderliness of nature has come about by chance.

They speak naturally, therefore, of the Architect, the Creator, the Intelligence at the heart of things—a Mind that is like the mind of a Great Mathematician, evidenced by the mathematical order of creation." (Fisk, *op. cit.*, pp. 90-91.)

Fisk continues, speaking of creation: "One cannot *reasonably* account for the world we have on the basis of planless accident. The hypothesis of a Creator-god is a *necessary* postulate. As the scientist, Arthur H. Compton, has put it: '. . . Evidence from both biological and physical science makes it difficult to escape the conclusion that our world is controlled by a supreme Intelligence which directs creation according to some great plan.' " (Ibid., pp. 96-97.)

It was Robert Millikan who said: "Nothing could be more antagonistic to the whole spirit of science [than atheism]. It seems to me that anyone who reflects at all believes one way or another in God." (Quoted in Fisk, *op. cit.*, p. 233.)

And Kirtley F. Mather, in *Science in Search of God*, is quoted as saying: "The more we know about the world in which we live, the better is our understanding of God, the truer our comprehension of His character. God is partially revealed by inanimate nature with its law abiding planets and its orderly chemical reactions. . . . But we find that power on a distinctly higher plane when we consider the lilies of the field or behold the fowls of the air. . . . Then when we investigate humanity and inquire into the nature of man, we greatly enlarge our estimate of the forces that can produce personality as well as organism." (New York: Henry Holt, 1928, pp. 74-75.)

Elmer Davis, widely known science writer, said in an article in *Harper's*, "So far from abolishing God, modern science—astrophysics in particular—comes near abolishing atheism." (*Harper's*, March 1930, p. 399.)

A. Cressy Morrison wrote a book on science and

religion, titled *Man Does Not Stand Alone*; and a condensed volume of this work was published by Reader's Digest Press. Morrison served as president of the New York Academy of Sciences and of the American Institute of the City of New York, and was a member of the executive board of the National Research Council, a fellow in the American Museum of Natural History, and a life member of the Royal Institution of Great Britain.

When the book was published, Clare Boothe Luce, noted woman journalist, said: "I think this book has made more converts from Atheism to Theism than thousands upon thousands of the church tracts that are spread upon the land the year around." The *Los Angeles Times* said: "The book's argument is well-nigh overwhelming . . . worth anyone's time." The *Christian Advocate* wrote: "Piling fact upon fact the author shows the absurdity of the atheistic point of view."

Among other things, Morrison wrote the following: "The first chapter of Genesis contains the real story of creation, and its essence has not been changed by knowledge acquired since it was written. This statement will cause a smile to develop on the genial face of the scientist and a look of incredulity but satisfaction from the true believer."

After discussing the creation of the animals and the herbs and the fact that "I have given every green herb for meat," he says:

"Here is a statement in biology that is most surprising, considering the time it was made. It is correct and in perfect accord with scientific knowledge. The statement about green herbs was not proved true until the synthesis of chlorophyl was discovered and the fact that all life was dependent on *every green thing* was made known by science. So is the order of procedure from chaos to man and his dominion. Can science pick a flaw in this briefest story ever told? The world's history in a few lines of print? The rest is detail. We must accord our homage to the writer, unknown and unheralded, in complete humility bow to his wisdom and admit his inspiraton. In the face of the simple truth here told, let us not quarrel over details due to translation and human interpolation or over the question of how God did his work or the time it took. Who knows? The facts as told have come down through the ages and *are facts*. . . .

"The scientist does not affirm, nor can he deny, the existence of Spirit or a Supreme Intelligence, yet in his inmost self he feels the impact of consciousness, thought, memory, and ideas emanating from that entity we call soul. He knows his inspiration does not come from matter. Science has no claim or right to the last word on the existence of a Supreme Intelligence until it can speak that word finally and forever." (A. Cressy Morrison, *Man Does Not Stand Alone*, Fleming H. Revell Co., 1944, pp. 103-104.)

Anthropologists in particular, but archaeologists and other scientists as well, freely use figures of high magnitude in estimating the age of life upon the earth, running anywhere from thousands to millions of years into the past. Much of the dating has been reached through the use of the radiocarbon method, which has been considered reliable for years by some scientists but which has been questioned repeatedly by others. Now comes a United Press International news release forcefully challenging the accuracy of that method for any period beyond 2,000 years B.C. The news article reads:

"Berrien Springs, Mich. (UPI) — A widely accepted method of determining the age of various sorts of life on earth back to 50,000 B.C. may be way off the mark for objects more than 4,000 years old, a physicist contends.

"Robert Brown, in a paper challenging the validity of the radiocarbon dating method, said he believes life on earth began about 5,000 B.C.—roughly the time some Bible scholars say the earth was created.

"Brown, director of the Geoscience Research Institute of Andrews University here, said the technique for determining the age of dead organisms has proven fairly accurate back to 2000 B.C.

"But, he said, data compiled during his 10-year study of the method suggests radioactive carbon atoms did not exist in the earth's atmosphere in measurable amounts before 2000 B.C., and therefore cannot be used to date objects prior to that time.

"Brown said he began his research with an initial skepticism of radiocarbon dating based on his belief in the Biblical accounts of creation and the universal flood.

" 'All we had in the past was speculation, which is the last desperate attempt of a believer to retain his faith without making it appear that he has turned his brain off,' he said.

"The radiocarbon method, developed shortly after World War II, involves measuring the radioactivity given off by the isotope carbon-14, which is produced in the air by cosmic rays striking air molecules and is absorbed by all living organisms.

"But, Brown said, rather than indicating a long period of radioactive decay, low radiocarbon levels could simply indicate some organisms started out with fewer radiocarbons.

"Conditions such as temperature of the planet and geomagnetic and solar magnetic fields belting the globe have altered atmospheric radiocarbons, causing carbon-14 dates to differ from real time, he said.

"At some point in time, he said, there were no radiocarbons in the atmosphere. Then, sometime before 2000 B.C., a major atmospheric change likely occurred resulting in a buildup of carbon-14 in the atmosphere over several centuries." (*Deseret News*, January 2, 1976.)

The history of the radiocarbon "time clock" is an interesting one. It was discovered by Dr. W. F. Libby, who received a Nobel prize for his work. As explained by Dr. Melvin A. Cook and M. Garfield Cook in their book *Science and Mormonism*, this "most reliable of all radioactive time clocks has been widely accepted in spite of a weakness recognized in the early days of its development by Dr. Libby himself. . . . Because it would take only about 30,000 years for radiocarbon to come close enough to overall equilibrium in the earth that an unbalance could not be detected experimentally, Dr. Libby chose to reject this evidence on the basis of what he considered to be common knowledge that the earth is not merely more than 30,000 years old but even billions of years old. One must have great faith in his theory to ignore experimental data in order to retain it. Dr. Libby adopted the *equilibrium model to read* his radioactive time clock; the evidence indicates that he should have adopted a nonequilibrium model in order to be consistent with the observed data and the other postulates of his radiocarbon model. Had he adopted the nonequilibrium model his method could still easily have been applied (and with relatively small differences for ages no greater than 4,000 years). However, it would have dated the whole atmosphere of the earth at roughly 10,000 years of age." (*Science and Mormonism*, 1967, p. 166.)

What a sweeping rejection this would have been to all the conjectured dates on the origin of life, which some would put back into millions of years!

It should be remembered that even the evolutionists admit that their evidence is largely conjectural, and that they deal in vast periods of time in which a million or two years seem to make little, if any, difference.

A recent edition of *Atlas of Ancient Archaeology*, for example, reads: "No one who reads newspapers can fail to know that there is now convincing evidence that the first steps in human evolution (the emergence of the hominid family) took place in Africa south of the Sahara. It seems that between four and three million years ago when the warm climate of the Pliocene Age was giving way to the much colder Pleistocene, primates in sub-Saharan Africa were evolving into the earliest 'men' or hominids."

The volume then describes the homo habilis, an offshoot of the hominids, which was "a little fellow averaging about four feet in height, but had a relatively large brain of about 700 cc, and is thought to have dominated, perhaps hunted and eaten, the surviving Australopithecines." (McGraw-Hill, 1975, pp. 7-8.) How could anyone know?

Note that "it is thought" that they did thus and so. This admission corresponds with another on the opposite page of this same book, in which the author admits "so little do we know," and "yet so uncertain is the evidence."

The endless evolutionary voyages into the seas of speculation certainly cannot be allowed to destroy our faith in divine revelation, which revelation completely refutes these hypotheses.

It should be remembered that just as there are many varying views on religion among the numerous churches, so there are also equally varying views among scientists.

It is a mistake to assume that there is *one* science, *one* united explanation for the origin of life, the origin of man, or the origin of the universe, for it just simply is not so.

There are imaginative researchers in science as there are in bibliology, and they do not all come up with the same answers. The very divergence of opinion among the researchers, anthropologists as well as others, is evidence in itself that there is no common ground on these matters among the scientists, earnest as they may be.

It is said to their credit that as honest men, they do adjust their thinking as new evidence presents itself. This, too, indicates that all have not yet found the final answer to man's origin nor to the beginning of life in any other field, although many, as above indicated, believe in the divine creation.

Since we have the sure word of revelation to guide us concerning creation, shall we exchange it for unproven hypotheses?

Shall we exchange solid truth for speculation?

God lives. Adam was the first man. He fell to provide mortality. Christ is God's Only Begotten Son. He died to give us resurrection and redemption.

Chapter Seven

ADAM NEXT TO CHRIST

❁

How do we explain "cave man" and "early man" and "stone age man"? They are simply a result of deterioration and retrogression. They fell away from a better life, that which was known to the first man, Adam.

There are "stone age" people living in the world right now in several areas, as reported by newspapers and magazines. How did they lapse into their present state? Are we going to say that they are only now evolving into humans who someday may become advanced like ourselves? What about the "pre-men" and early cultures?

Retrogression is the only dependable explanation. See what scripture has to say about the true first man:

"And I, God, created man in mine own image, in the image of mine Only Begotten created I him; male and female created I them." (Moses 2:27.) His image certainly was not to be found in apes or missing links or worms or amoebas!

Think for a moment about the Only Begotten Son of God. He was Jesus the Christ—Creator, Redeemer, and Savior. How did he appear to men? Remember that we were made after his image. He was the pattern of our existence. He was our physical prototype as well as our great spiritual example, the model for our lives.

We were born on earth as babies, just as he was. We shall go to the grave as he did. We shall be in the likeness of his resurrection. In every way he is our physical prototype, from beginning to end. And God is the Father of us all.

The Almighty, in creating various forms of life, commanded all to reproduce after their own kind. Man also was commanded to reproduce himself. He could bring forth only after his kind according to the law of God, and he was "after the kind" or order of his Eternal Father in heaven. No lower forms were involved.

When the Almighty spoke of lower forms of life that he created, he said this: "And it became a living soul also. . . . *for it remaineth in the sphere in which I, God, created it*, yea, even all things which I prepared for the use of man." (Moses 3:9. Italics added.)

This is interesting in view of the previous scripture in which all life was commanded to reproduce *only* after its own kind. Now he says that all forms of life remained in the sphere in which he created them. There was no transfer from one species to another.

This also is interesting:

"And out of the ground I, the Lord God, formed every beast of the field, and every fowl of the air; and commanded that they should come unto Adam, to see what he would call them; and they were also living souls; for I, God, breathed into them the breath of life, and commanded that whatsoever Adam called every living creature, that should be the name thereof.

"And Adam gave names to all cattle, and to the fowl of the air, and to every beast of the field. . . ." (Moses 3:19-20.)

Experts in the life sciences know that such a task would require great intelligence. No "pre-man" could do that.

The scripture goes on: " . . . Adam began to till the earth, and to have dominion over all the beasts of the field, and to eat his bread by the sweat of his brow, as I the Lord had commanded him. And Eve, also, his wife, did labor with him." (Moses 5:1.)

Then when did agriculture begin? It was not an

evolution at all, as some anthropologists have written. Agriculture began with the first man, simultaneously with his expulsion from the Garden of Eden, simultaneously with his transition from what Dr. James E. Talmage calls an immortal state (not subject to death) to mortality. Actually, a type of agriculture began before Adam's fall, for "the Lord God, took the man, and put him into the Garden of Eden, to dress it, and to keep it." (Moses 3:15.) So Adam was a farmer to begin with.

Man had to eat, and now, being mortal, he had to do so by the sweat of his brow. He had to work, till the ground, and domesticate animals so that some of them would work also. That was in the very beginning and was not part of some later development, as is claimed.

Not only did Adam and Eve become farmers, but they taught their sons likewise, and they also became farmers and stockmen. Note the scripture: "Abel was a keeper of sheep, but Cain was a tiller of the ground." (Moses 5:17.) It was to obtain the flocks of Abel that Cain slew his brother, for he said: " . . . surely the flocks of my brother falleth into my hands." (Moses 5:33.)

So the first men knew agriculture. Adam had a numerous posterity. Would they not earn their living much as he did?

Now, who was Adam?

"And the first man of all men have I called Adam, which is many." (Moses 1:34.)

Keep in mind that although this information is taken from the writings of Moses, it was not given to Joseph Smith by manuscript nor by translation of some ancient record. It was given to him by the Lord as *modern revelation*. So it is fact, not mythology in any sense.

In other revelations given to Joseph Smith we have the same information. When the Lord traced the line of the priesthood, he said: "And from Enoch to Abel, who was slain by the conspiracy of his brother [the Cain and Abel story therefore was likewise true and not fable], who received the priesthood by the commandments of God, by the hand of his father Adam, *who was the first man*—Which priesthood continueth in the church of God in all generations, and is without beginning of days or end of years." (D&C 84:16-17. Italics added.)

Let us face it. This is modern revelation. This is God speaking, and he is thus telling us so that "we henceforth be no more children, tossed to and fro, and carried about with every wind of doctrine, by the sleight of men, and cunning craftiness"—or, as the revised version of the Bible says, "after the wiles of error." (Ephesians 4:14.)

As Adam was the first man, so Eve was the first woman; and by revelation to the Prophet Joseph Smith, we have the fact that she was the "first of all women." In the fourth chapter of the book of Moses in the Pearl of Great Price, we find the following: "And Adam called his wife's name Eve, because she was the mother of all living; for thus have I, the Lord God, called the first of all women, which are many." (Moses 4:26.)

So we readily see, then, by actual revelation from God to Joseph Smith that not only was she the first woman, but she was also "the mother of all living" human beings. Inasmuch as we are given this great fact by revelation, it should clarify many important questions in our minds and eliminate uncertainties that arise from the teachings of uninspired men.

Adam and his family lived very much as people do today. They worked for a living. They had their good times and their bad times. Some of their children were obedient; others were not. As Adam taught them the gospel, Satan came also and influenced some of them contrariwise. But:

". . . Adam hearkened unto the voice of God, and called upon his sons to repent.

"And then began these men to call upon the name

56

of the Lord, and the Lord blessed them;

"And a book of remembrance was kept, in the which was recorded, in the language of Adam, for it was given unto as many as called upon God to write by the spirit of inspiration;

"And by them their children were taught to read and write, having a language which was pure and undefiled." (Moses 6:1, 4-6.)

And what was more, these early men—highly intelligent and taught by inspiration of God—became genealogists also. This was one of the important duties that the Lord laid upon them; and not only did they write genealogy and family history (their book of remembrance), but they even kept a careful record of their ordinations.

"Now this prophecy Adam spake as he was moved upon by the Holy Ghost, and a genealogy was kept of the children of God. And this was the book of the generations of Adam. . . ." (Moses 6:8.)

Said President Joseph Fielding Smith: "Adam was placed here, not a wild, half-civilized savage, but a perfectly developed man, with wonderful intelligence, for he helped to create this earth. He was chosen in pre-existence to be the first man upon the earth and the father of the human race, and he will preside over his posterity forever.

"Now, the Lord did not choose a being that had just developed from the lower forms of life, to be a prince, an archangel, to preside over the human race forever! Adam, as Michael, was one of the greatest intelligences in the spirit world and he stands next to Jesus Christ. When he came upon the earth, the Lord gave him a perfect form of government.

"The first man placed upon this earth was an intelligent being, created in the image of God, possessed of wisdom and knowledge, with power to communicate his thoughts in a language, both oral and written, which was superior to anything to be found on the earth today. This may sound very sweeping and dogmatic to those who hold to the other view, but it is not any more so than their statements to the contrary. Moreover, I do not say it of myself, but merely repeat what the Lord has said; and surely the Creator, above all others, ought to know!

"The first man was instructed by the best teacher man ever had, for he was taught of God, and spoke the language of the Most High, in which angels conversed. This language he taught to his children. It is true that he was left to work out, through the use of his faculties, many of nature's great secrets; but the Lord did not leave him helpless, but instructed him, and he was inspired by the Spirit of the Lord.

"The Lord gave him commandments after he was driven out of the Garden of Eden, revealed to him the plan of salvation, and he taught his children, and he set up a government. It was a perfect government, for Adam listened to the counsels of the Almighty, his Father, and our Father. He taught his children principles of divine truth and endeavored to establish them in the knowledge and understanding of the things of the kingdom of God.

"Some people have the idea that the Ten Commandments were first given by Moses when he directed the children of Israel and formulated their code of laws. This is not the case. These great commandments are from the beginning and were understood in righteous communities in the days of Adam. They are, in fact, fundamental parts of the gospel of Jesus Christ, and the gospel in its fulness was first given to Adam." (*Doctrines of Salvation*, 1:94-96.)

The anthropologists tell us that religion among early men evolved from superstitions. But how far afield they are! Religion was *revealed* by God to the very first man, whom he ordained to be a high priest and to whom he gave the First Presidency! First Presidency of what? Why, of the Church of Jesus Christ, the only organization in which there is a true First Presidency, with the divine keys and powers thereof. (*Teachings of the Prophet Joseph Smith*, p. 157.)

The Prophet Joseph says that "the Priesthood is an everlasting principle, and existed with God from eternity. . . . The keys have to be brought from heaven whenever the Gospel is sent. When they are revealed from heaven, it is by Adam's authority."

And why?

Because Adam stands next to Christ in authority and was the first man to receive the keys of the First Presidency. (*Teachings*, pp. 157-58.)

The Prophet, again speaking of Adam as the first man, said that he "is spoken of in Daniel as being the 'Ancient of Days,' or in other words, the first and the oldest of all, the great, grand progenitor of whom it is said in another place he is Michael, because he was the first and father of all, not only by progeny, but the first to hold the spiritual blessings, to whom was made known the plan of ordinances for the salvation of his posterity unto the end, and to whom Christ was first revealed, and through whom Christ has been revealed from heaven, and will continue to be revealed from henceforth. Adam holds the keys of the dispensation of the fullness of times; i.e., the dispensation of all the times have been and will be revealed through him from the beginning to Christ, and from Christ to the end of the dispensations that are to be revealed." (*Teachings*, p. 167.)

So not only were Adam and his family intelligent persons, but they were given the revelations of God, *who taught them*. The Church was organized among them, and the priesthood was bestowed upon them to give validity to all they did.

The genealogy of the Savior as provided in Luke calls Adam a son of God. (Luke 3:38.) So does the revelation given to Joseph Smith: "And this is the genealogy of the sons of Adam, who was the son of God, with whom God, himself, conversed. And they were preachers of righteousness, and spake and prophesied, and called upon all men, everywhere, to repent; and faith was taught unto the children of men." (Moses 6:22-23.)

We need to understand the true concept of the first man, Adam. He was next to Christ in authority in the creation; he still is. He directs all dispensations of the gospel ever given to mankind, as the Prophet Joseph Smith taught.

He was a preacher of righteousness to his family. Holding the keys of the First Presidency, he presided over the Church of Christ in his day, for the Church was organized among his descendants. He was taught the gospel from the beginning of his mortality. He was baptized, even as we are, and received the gift of the Holy Ghost, even as we do:

"And it came to pass, when the Lord had spoken with Adam, our father, that Adam cried unto the Lord, and he was caught away by the Spirit of the Lord, and was carried down into the water, and was laid under the water, and was brought forth out of the water.

"And thus he was baptized, and the Spirit of God descended upon him, and thus he was born of the Spirit, and became quickened in the inner man.

"And he heard a voice out of heaven, saying: Thou art baptized with fire, and with the Holy Ghost. This is the record of the Father, and the Son, from henceforth and forever." (Moses 6:64-68.)

Here is an important point. Note these words, "This is the record of the Father, and the Son, from henceforth and forever." The Father and the Son here bore record that Adam, who was a *third* party and who in the preexistence was Michael, but now in mortality was Adam, was baptized for the remission of the sin he committed in the Garden of Eden. Verse 53 of that chapter specifically says that in baptism Adam received a remission of his sin:

"And our father Adam spake unto the Lord, and said: Why is it that men must repent and be baptized in water? And the Lord said unto Adam: *Behold I have forgiven thee thy transgression in the Garden of Eden*." (Italics added.)

This is a remarkable statement. Baptism now gave to Adam freedom from blame for the fall. But it did not remove the penalty of his sin, which was mortality and eventual death. The resurrection of the Savior was provided to overcome death and turn mortality into immortality. Baptism does not do that. But it was baptism that cleansed Adam of guilt, so that again he could commune freely with the Lord.

This leads us to some serious questions: Some say that Adam was God the Eternal Father. Yet Adam sinned. Does God sin? Would our God and Father require baptism to free him from *sin?* Shall we say that God the Father could—or did—sin? If God were to sin, would he not cease to be God?

So again the Adam-God fable is shown to be a ridiculous contradiction.

The name of Christ was revealed to Adam as he was given the gospel, and the plan of redemption was made known to him. Note again the record of scripture:

"But God hath made known unto our fathers that all men must repent.

"And he called upon our father Adam by his own voice, saying: I am God; I made the world, and men before they were in the flesh.

"And he also said unto him: If thou wilt turn unto me, and hearken unto my voice, and believe, and repent of all thy transgressions, and be baptized, even in water, in the name of mine Only Begotten Son, who is full of grace and truth, which is Jesus Christ, the only name which shall be given under heaven, whereby salvation shall come unto the children of men, ye shall receive the gift of the Holy Ghost, asking all things in his name, and whatsoever ye shall ask, it shall be given you.

"And our father Adam spake unto the Lord, and said: Why is it that men must repent and be baptized in water? And the Lord said unto Adam: Behold I have forgiven thee thy transgression in the Garden of Eden.

"Hence came the saying abroad among the people, That the Son of God hath atoned for original guilt, wherein the sins of the parents cannot be answered upon the heads of the children, for they are whole from the foundation of the world." (Moses 6:50-54.)

The original sin of Adam was one thing, but the sins that we individually commit are something else again. We must assume the full responsibility for our own acts. If we sin, we do so as free agents. As one of our Articles of Faith says: "We believe that men will be punished for their own sins, and not for Adam's transgression."

Without free agency there could be no gospel of Christ. The character development provided by the gospel will lead us to the perfection of which the Savior spoke in the Sermon on the Mount only if we elect to live the gospel. Otherwise we can never receive of its benefits. (Alma 12:18.) That right of election—that right of free agency—must ever be preserved. If a man commits sin, he must have the liberty to turn from his ways and repent, and thus come under the purview of the gospel.

Hence the gospel is called the "perfect law of liberty" (James 1:25), and those who are blessed by it enjoy the "glorious liberty of the children of God" (Romans 8:21).

When Paul addressed the Corinthians he said: " . . . where the Spirit of the Lord is, there is liberty." (2 Corinthians 3:17.) This was reflected in the Book of Mormon statement that "the Spirit of God . . . is also the Spirit of freedom." (Alma 61:15.) Isaiah predicted that freedom would characterize the labors of the Savior, who confirmed it as he ministered in Palestine. (Isaiah 61:1; Luke 4:18.)

Understanding the importance of free agency, and knowing that his children would have the opportunity of choosing right from wrong, Adam preached repentance in his day. Free agency was cherished by his family. It was preserved by the Lord himself, who said:

"And it is given unto them to know good from evil; wherefore they are agents unto themselves, and I have given unto you another law and commandment.

"Wherefore teach it unto your children, that all men, everywhere, must repent, or they can in nowise inherit the kingdom of God, for no unclean thing can dwell there, or dwell in his presence; for, in the language of Adam, Man of Holiness is his name, and the name of his Only Begotten is the Son of Man, even Jesus Christ, a righteous Judge, who shall come in the meridian of time.

"Therefore I give unto you a commandment, to teach these things freely unto your children, saying:

"That by reason of transgression cometh the fall, which fall bringeth death, and inasmuch as ye were born into the world by water, and blood, and the spirit, which I have made, and so became of dust a living soul, even so ye must be born again into the kingdom of heaven, of water, and of the Spirit, and be cleansed by blood, even the blood of mine Only Begotten; that ye might be sanctified from all sin, and enjoy the words of eternal life in this world, and eternal life in the world to come, even immortal glory;

"For by the water ye keep the commandment; by the Spirit ye are justified, and by the blood ye are sanctified;

"Therefore it is given to abide in you; the record of heaven; the Comforter; the peaceable things of immortal glory; the truth of all things; that which quickeneth all things, which maketh alive all things; that which knoweth all things, and hath all power according to wisdom, mercy, truth, justice, and judgment.

"And now, behold, I say unto you: This is the plan

of salvation unto all men, through the blood of mine Only Begotten, who shall come in the meridian of time." (Moses 6:56-62.)

These scriptures answer every speculation of the anthropologists who say that all religion evolved, that even Judaism evolved, and that eventually Christianity did likewise.

The gospel was first preached to us in our preexistent life. There the plan of salvation was unfolded. Christ was chosen as the Redeemer in that pristine period, and as we accepted him there, all the hosts of heaven shouted for joy. (Job 38.) The program of the Lord was fully explained to us at that time, for we were intelligent people as pre-earth spirits, and we were organized there before the world was. Then we were transferred from one intelligent existence (pre-earth) to another (mortality) here on earth.

We have this interesting information:

"Now the Lord had shown unto me, Abraham, the intelligences that were organized before the world was; and among all these there were many of the noble and great ones;

"And God saw these souls that they were good, and he stood in the midst of them, and he said: These I will make my rulers; for he stood among those that were spirits, and he saw that they were good; and he said unto me: Abraham, thou art one of them; thou wast chosen before thou wast born.

"And there stood one among them that was like unto God, and he said unto those who were with him: We will go down, for there is space there, and we will take of these materials, and we will make an earth whereon these may dwell;

"And we will prove them herewith, to see if they will do all things whatsoever the Lord their God shall command them;

"And they who keep their first estate shall be added upon; and they who keep not their first estate shall not have glory in the same kingdom with those who keep their first estate; and they who keep their second estate shall have glory added upon their heads for ever and ever.

"And the Lord said: Whom shall I send? And one answered like unto the Son of Man: Here am I, send me. And another answered and said: Here am I, send me. And the Lord said: I will send the first.

"And the second was angry, and kept not his first estate; and, at that day, many followed after him." (Abraham 3:22-28.)

Further light is given in Moses:

"And I, the Lord God, spake unto Moses, saying: That Satan, whom thou hast commanded in the name of mine Only Begotten, is the same which was from the beginning, and he came before me, saying—Behold, here am I, send me, I will be thy son, and I will redeem all mankind, that one soul shall not be lost, and surely I will do it; wherefore give me thine honor.

"But, behold, my Beloved Son, which was my Beloved and Chosen from the beginning, said unto me — Father, thy will be done, and the glory be thine forever.

"Wherefore, because that Satan rebelled against me, and sought to destroy the agency of man, which I, the Lord God, had given him, and also, that I should give unto him mine own power; by the power of mine Only Begotten, I caused that he should be cast down;

"And he became Satan, yea, even the devil, the father of all lies, to deceive and to blind men, and to lead them captive at his will, even as many as would not hearken unto my voice." (Moses 4:1-4.)

We need to see the true picture of Adam and his family, and of the Lord and his plan for us.

All was prepared in the beginning. There was no slow development of human beings on earth. They were placed here suddenly in the form of Adam and Eve. Let us realize that these two people were among the chief intelligences and most advanced children of God in the pre-earth life. Jesus was chosen as the Redeemer, *but Adam stands next to him.*

Adam, this first man, was a chosen instrument of God and has been from the eternities. When it came time for God to populate this earth, he sent the one great and significant being who stood next in line to Jehovah as the one to come here first. He was no groveling cave man or pre-man or missing link. *He stood next to God.* He was the Archangel among all the hosts of heaven. He was highly intelligent, taught by God, guided by God, and ordained of God.

The Church of Jesus Christ was organized among his family, and Adam was made the earthly head of it. He is still the next officer in the church — for all eternity — under Christ. As Joseph Smith said, Adam presides over all the dispensations, and whenever dispensations of the gospel have been given to the earth by the Savior, it has been done through Adam and by the authority given to Adam by the Savior.

Adam was and is a tremendous individual. He has been grossly misunderstood. Even by the religionists he has been downgraded and minimized.

Jesus himself is often misunderstood, being referred to as only the babe of Bethlehem who commenced his career as a child born in a stable, later becoming an itinerant preacher in Palestine.

Adam is similarly misunderstood, being berated for his original sin, and equated with cave men and missing links, or still worse, with some primordial worm or microbe.

Christ is God — the Creator — and with his Father is the greatest of all. But Adam stands next to him, and never let that be forgotten.

Chapter Eight

THE ORIGINAL SIN

A misunderstanding of the original sin of Adam has caused no end of anguish on the part of parents who have lost little children who were not sprinkled in so-called baptism. It has caused mental distress likewise on the part of many others who have seen the inconsistency of the creeds usually taught in sectarian churches on this subject.

The doctrine of original sin goes back to the Council of Carthage of the Catholic Church, held in 418 A.D. It was stressed again at the Council of Orange in 529 and at the Council of Trent in 1546.

Although the doctrine is primarily a Catholic one, it has found its way into the creeds of some of the Protestant churches as well. A number of the Protestant churches baptize infants by sprinkling, but others reject baptism altogether, infant or adult, not regarding it as necessary for salvation.

Methodists are in the middle of the situation, as are the Presbyterians. Both are willing to allow baptism, by either sprinkling, pouring, or immersion, and they do baptize infants when the parents desire it. But both say that baptism is not really necessary.

The clearest definition of "original sin" in the context of sectarian churches of course comes from the Roman Catholics. The book *Catholic Belief*, as revised by Canon Joseph Cartmell, D.D., written under the imprimatur of the Roman church, and published in Great Britain in 1957, says of original sin: "The Church teaches . . . that all men, naturally descended from Adam (Our Lady alone excepted) [it is the belief of that church that Mary the mother of Christ was exempt from original sin], have contracted the guilt of original sin; in other words, that they come into this world deprived of the sanctity and justice which God intended them to have. . . . Original sin is a state of sin which we inherit." (London: Burns Oates and Washbourne, Ltd., 1957, p. 7.)

The *Question Box*, published by the Roman church to answer questions raised by Protestants, says of original sin: "It was a grievous sin, because Adam could easily have avoided it, as there was in him neither ignorance nor concupiscence [a strong or ardent desire], and he certainly knew, as head of the race, what terrible consequences would follow for all mankind." (P. 219.)

Baptism is mistakenly declared to be the means of escape from the blemish of original sin.

It is appalling how greatly the sectarian people misunderstand the fall of Adam. As previously quoted, the Book of Mormon makes it abundantly clear that the fall was part of the divine plan, a necessity, and that without it there would have been no human race, for Adam and Eve were physically unable to have children in their paradisiacal condition.

Not only is the sectarian view of original sin based on a complete misunderstanding of the true doctrine concerning the fall, but it is equally a mistake to suppose that baptism was provided to remove the effects of the original sin.

The scripture is very clear in stating that if Adam and Eve were to partake of the forbidden fruit, death would result. Therefore, death was the penalty for the original sin, and baptism does not overcome death. The Savior's resurrection did that.

" . . . in the day that thou eatest thereof thou shalt surely die," says the King James Bible (Genesis 2:17), in explaining the sin of Adam and Eve.

Or as the Torah of the Jews expresses it: "Of every tree of the garden you are free to eat, but as for the tree of knowledge of good and bad, you must not eat of it, for as soon as you eat of it, you shall die."

The Jerusalem Bible, a recent Catholic version, has this rendering of the passage in question: "You may eat indeed of all the trees in the garden. Nevertheless of the tree of the knowledge of good and evil you are not to eat, for on the day you eat it you shall most surely die."

The Complete Bible, An American Translation, by Smith and Goodspeed, reads: "From every tree in the garden you are free to eat; but from the tree of the knowledge of good and evil you must not eat; for the day that you eat of it, you shall certainly die."

Another Roman Catholic Bible, translated by Mons. Knox, using the Vulgate as a base after comparisons with Hebrew and Greek texts, and published in England in 1955, reads: "Thou mayest eat thy fill of all the trees in the garden except the tree which brings knowledge of good and evil; if ever thou eatest of this, thy doom is death."

The Living Bible, Billy Graham Crusade Edition, reads: "You may eat any fruit in the garden except from the Tree of Conscience—for its fruit will open your eyes to make you aware of right and wrong, good and bad. If you eat its fruit, you will be doomed to die."

Other new translations might be quoted on this text, but all agree: death was the penalty for eating from that tree.

The book of Moses, which was given by revelation to the Prophet Joseph Smith and therefore was not subject to any mistakes in translation, reads:

"And I, the Lord God, commanded the man, saying, Of every tree of the garden thou mayest freely eat,

"But of the tree of the knowledge of good and evil, thou shalt not eat of it, nevertheless, thou mayest choose for thyself, for it is given unto thee; but, remember that I forbid it, for in the day thou eatest thereof thou shalt surely die." (Moses 3:16-17.)

This is all confirmed by what Eve said as the devil tempted her to violate the command of God. Says the King James Version:

"Now the serpent was more subtil than any beast of the field which the Lord God had made. And he said unto the woman, Yea, hath God said, Ye shall not eat of every tree of the garden?

"And the woman said unto the serpent, We may eat of the fruit of the trees of the garden:

"But of the fruit of the tree which is in the midst of the garden, God hath said, Ye shall not eat of it, neither shall ye touch it, lest ye die.

"And the serpent said unto the woman, Ye shall not surely die:

"For God doth know that in the day ye eat thereof, then your eyes shall be opened, and ye shall be as the gods, knowing good and evil." (Genesis 3:1-5.)

The Jerusalem Bible reads:

"The serpent was the most subtle of all the wild beast that Yahweh God had made. It asked the woman, 'Did God really say you were not to eat from any trees in the garden?'

"The woman answered the serpent, 'We may eat the fruit of the trees in the garden.

" 'But of the fruit of the tree in the middle of the garden God said, "You must not eat it, nor touch it, under pain of death." '

"Then the serpent said to the woman, 'No! You will not die! God knows in fact that on the day you eat it, your eyes will be opened and you will be like the gods, knowing good and evil."

An American Translation by Smith and Goodspeed reads:

"Now the serpent was the most clever of all the wild beasts that the Lord God had made.

70

" 'And so God has said that you are not to eat from any tree of the garden?' he said to the woman.

" 'From the fruit of the trees of the garden we may eat,' the woman said to the serpent; 'it is only concerning the fruit of the tree which is in the middle of the garden that God has said, "You may not eat of it, nor touch it, lest you die." '

"But the serpent said to the woman,

" 'You would not die at all; for God knows that the very day you eat of it, your eyes will be opened, and you will be like gods who know good from evil.' "

The Knox Catholic Bible reads:

"Of all the beasts which the Lord God had made, there was none that could match the serpent in cunning. It was he who said to the woman, What is this command God has given you, not to eat the fruit of any tree in the garden?

"To which the woman answered, We can eat the fruit of any tree in the garden except the tree in the middle of it; it is this God has forbidden us to eat or even touch, on pain of death.

"And the serpent said to her, What is this talk of death? God knows well that as soon as you eat this fruit your eyes will be opened, and you yourselves will be like gods, knowing good and evil."

And Billy Graham's Bible says:

"The serpent was the craftiest of all the creatures the Lord God had made. So the serpent came to the woman. 'Really?' he asked. '*None* of the fruit in the garden? God says you mustn't eat *any* of it?'

" 'Of course we may eat it,' the woman told him. 'It's only the fruit from the tree at the center of the garden that we are not to eat. God says we mustn't eat it or even touch it, or we will die.'

" 'That's a lie!' the serpent hissed. 'You'll not die! God knows very well that the instant you eat it you will become like him, for your eyes will be opened — you will be able to distinguish good from evil.' "

Other modern translations follow the identical line. All say that death was the result of the fall.

Our book of Moses, again by revelation, says:

"And now the serpent was more subtle than any beast of the field which I, the Lord God, had made.

"And Satan put it into the heart of the serpent, (for he had drawn away many after him,) and he sought also to beguile Eve, for he knew not the mind of God, wherefore he sought to destroy the world.

"And he said unto the woman, Yea, hath God said — Ye shall not eat of every tree of the garden? (And he spake by the mouth of the serpent.)

"And the woman said unto the serpent: We may eat of the fruit of the trees of the garden;

"But of the fruit of the tree which thou beholdest in the midst of the garden, God hath said — Ye shall not eat of it, neither shall ye touch it, lest ye die.

"And the serpent said unto the woman, Ye shall not surely die;

"For God doth know that in the day ye eat thereof, then your eyes shall be opened, and ye shall be as gods, knowing good and evil." (Moses 4:5-11.)

With the facts before us, as contained in the various versions of the scriptures, and particularly in the revelation known as the book of Moses in our Pearl of Great Price, can anyone fail to see that it is death which resulted from the fall?

And what removes death? Baptism? Hardly.

It was Christ's atonement and resurrection that overcame death. Baptism had nothing to do with it. All people, baptized or not, Christian or not, Jewish or not, gentile or not, will be resurrected by the power of Christ.

Paul expressed it: "As in Adam all die, even so in Christ shall all be made alive." (1 Corinthians 15:22.)

Paul also discoursed on the relationship of Adam to Christ, and of the fall to the redemption, and said:

"Now if Christ be preached that he rose from the

dead, how say some among you that there is no resurrection of the dead?

"But if there be no resurrection of the dead, then is Christ not risen;

"And if Christ be not risen, then is our preaching vain, and your faith is also vain.

"Yea, and we are found false witnesses of God; because we have testified of God that he raised up Christ: whom he raised not up, if so be that the dead rise not.

"For if the dead rise not, then is not Christ raised:

"And if Christ be not raised, your faith is vain; ye are yet in your sins.

"Then they also which are falleth asleep in Christ are perished.

"If in this life only we have hope in Christ, we are of all men most miserable.

"But now is Christ risen from the dead, and become the firstfruits of them that slept.

"For since by man came death, by man came also the resurrection of the dead.

"For as in Adam all die, even so in Christ shall all be made alive." (1 Corinthians 15:12-22.)

It is obvious, then, how widely the churches of the world have strayed from the truth with regard to Adam, the fall, Christ and the resurrection, and the true doctrine of baptism for the remission of sins. Baptism was given to remit our personal sins as well as to grant us admission into the Church. It has nothing to do with either Adam's sin or death or the resurrection.

Our second Article of Faith is directed to this point: "We believe that men will be punished for their own sins, and not for Adam's transgression."

No stain is left upon any of us because of Adam's sin. We are born pure and innocent before God. In fact, he regards us as being unaccountable for sins until we reach the age of eight years. This is a far cry from infant baptism and its alleged purpose.

Note what the Lord says in modern revelation:

"But behold, I say unto you, that little children are redeemed from the foundation of the world through Mine Only Begotten;

"Wherefore, they cannot sin, for power is not given unto Satan to tempt little children, until they begin to become accountable before me." (D&C 29:46-47.)

"But little children are holy, being sanctified through the atonement of Jesus Christ; and this is what the scriptures mean." (D&C 74:7.)

The Lord also said: "Every spirit of man was innocent in the beginning; and God having redeemed man from the fall, men became again, in their infant state, innocent before God." (D&C 93:38.)

And then he said:

"And again, inasmuch as parents have children in Zion, or in any of her stakes which are organized, that teach them not to understand the doctrine of repentance, faith in Christ the Son of the living God, and of baptism and the gift of the Holy Ghost by the laying on of the hands, when eight years old, the sin be upon the heads of the parents.

"For this shall be a law unto the inhabitants of Zion, or in any of her stakes which are organized.

"And their children shall be baptized for the remission of their sins when eight years old, and receive the laying on of the hands.

"And they shall also teach their children to pray, and to walk uprightly before the Lord." (D&C 68:25-28.)

Adam served the purpose of God in his capacity, even as did Christ in his vital role. It was all in the plan of the Lord.

Regarding the fall, President Joseph Fielding Smith said:

"Before partaking of the fruit Adam could have lived forever; therefore, his status was one of immortality. When he ate, he became subject to death, and therefore he became mortal. This was a transgression of the law, but not a sin in the strict sense, for it was something that Adam and Eve had to do!

"I am sure that neither Adam nor Eve looked upon it as a sin, when they learned the consequences, and this is discovered in their words after they learned the consequences.

"Adam said: *'Blessed be the name of God, for because of my transgression my eyes are opened, and in this life I shall have joy, and again in the flesh I shall see God.'*

"Eve said: *'Were it not for our transgression we never should have had seed, and never should have known good and evil, and the joy of our redemption, and the eternal life which God giveth unto all the obedient.'* [Moses 5:10-11.]

"We can hardly look upon anything resulting in such benefits as being a sin, in the sense in which we consider sin." (*Doctrines of Salvation*, 1:115.)

President Smith also said:

"The gospel teaches us that if Adam and Eve had not partaken of that fruit of the tree of the knowledge of good and evil, they would have remained in the Garden of Eden in that same condition prevailing before the fall. Under those conditions they would have had no seed. *'Adam fell that men might be'* as it was decreed in the heavens before the world was. Lehi has given us a very clear and comprehensive view of the mission of Adam and of the atonement of Jesus Christ, and the Book of Mormon is very explicit in teaching these fundamental doctrines. In regard to the pre-mortal condition of Adam and the entire earth, Lehi has stated the following:

" 'And now, behold, if Adam had not transgressed he would not have fallen, but he would have remained in the garden of Eden. And *all things which were created must have remained in the same state in which they were after they were created; and they must have remained forever, and had no end.'* [2 Nephi 2:19-26.]

"Is not this statement plain enough? Whom are you going to believe, the Lord, or men?

"The Lord did not intend the earth to stay in that condition. Lehi further says: 'But behold, *all things have been done in the wisdom of him who knoweth all things.*' This earth was prepared for the advancement of the children of God. We came from the pre-existence to receive tabernacles of flesh and bones and to pass through mortality. It was decreed in the heavens that men should die after coming into this probation and learning the pains and tribulations of mortality as well as its joys and happiness. Jesus Christ is spoken of in the scriptures as the Lamb slain from the foundation of the world. [Revelation 13:8.] Peter says we were not redeemed with corruptible things, as silver and gold, but with the precious blood of Christ, as of a lamb without blemish, 'Who verily was forordained before the foundation of the world, but was manifest in these last times for you.' [1 Peter 1:20.] So the plan of salvation was all understood in the world of spirits, and we were taught the purpose of mortal life which Adam should bring into the earth.

"By revelation we are well informed that *Adam was not subject to death when he was placed in the Garden of Eden, nor was there any death upon the earth.* The Lord has not seen fit to tell us definitely just how Adam came for we are not ready to receive that truth. He did not come here a resurrected being to die again for we are taught most clearly that those who pass through the resurrection receive immortality, and can die no more.

"It is sufficient for us to know, until the Lord reveals more about it, that Adam was not subject to death but had the power, through transgressing the law, to become subject to death and to cause the same curse to come upon the earth and all life upon it. For this earth, once pronounced good, was cursed after the fall. It is passing through its mortal probation as well as the life which is upon it, and will eventually receive the resurrection and a place of exaltation which is decreed in the heavens for it." (*Doctrines of Salvation*, 1:109-10.)

Chapter Nine

INFANT BAPTISM

Baptism of infants was not a part of the gospel as it was taught by the Savior. Instead of condemning them, he said: "Suffer little children, and forbid them not, to come unto me: for of such is the kingdom of heaven." (Matthew 19:14.)

Being of the kingdom of heaven, and not being held accountable for their acts until they reach eight years of age, they are not required to have any of the saving ordinances of the gospel. They already are of the kingdom of heaven, and there is nothing better. Hence, when little children die, they go directly to our Father in heaven, as the Prophet Joseph Smith said:

"All who have died without a knowledge of this Gospel, who would have received it if they had been permitted to tarry, shall be heirs of the celestial kingdom of God; also all that shall die henceforth without a knowledge of it, who would have received it with all their hearts, shall be heirs of that kingdom, for I, the Lord, will judge all men according to their works, according to the desire of their hearts. And I also beheld that all children who die before they arrive at the years of accountability, are saved in the celestial kingdom of heaven." (*Teachings*, p. 107.)

At another time the Prophet spoke of the death of little children and gave this view:

"The Lord takes many away even in infancy, that they may escape the envy of man, and the sorrows and evils of this present world; they were too pure, too lovely, to live on earth; therefore, if rightly considered, instead of mourning we have reason to rejoice as they

are delivered from evil, and we shall soon have them
again." (*Teachings*, pp. 196-97.)

The most pointed thing we have in all holy writ
directed against infant baptism appears in the Book of
Mormon, wherein the prophet Mormon says:

"My beloved son, Moroni, I rejoice exceedingly
that your Lord Jesus Christ hath been mindful of you,
and hath called you to his ministry, and to his holy
work.

"I am mindful of you always in my prayers, continually praying unto God the Father in the name of his
Holy Child, Jesus, that he, through his infinite good-
ness and grace, will keep you through the endurance of
faith on his name to the end.

"And now, my son, I speak unto you concerning
that which grieveth me exceedingly; for it grieveth me
that there should disputations rise among you.

"For, if I have learned the truth, there have been
disputations among you concerning the baptism of your
little children.

"And now, my son, I desire that ye should labor
diligently that this gross error should be removed from
among you; for, for this intent I have written this
epistle.

"For immediately after I had learned these things
of you I inquired of the Lord concerning the matter.
And the word of the Lord came to me by the power of
the Holy Ghost, saying:

"Listen to the words of Christ, your Redeemer,
your Lord and your God. Behold, I came into the world
not to call the righteous but sinners to repentance; the
whole need no physician, but they that are sick; wherefore, little children are whole, for they are not capable
of committing sin; wherefore the curse of Adam is taken
from them in me, that it hath no power over them; and
the law of circumcision is done away in me.

"And after this manner did the Holy Ghost manifest the word of God unto me; wherefore, my beloved

son, I know that it is solemn mockery before God that ye should baptize little children.

"Behold I say unto you that this thing shall ye teach — repentance and baptism unto those who are accountable and capable of committing sin; yea, teach parents that they must repent and be baptized, and humble themselves as their little children, and they shall all be saved with their little children.

"And their little children need no repentance, neither baptism. Behold, baptism is unto repentance to the fulfilling the commandments unto the remission of sins.

"But little children are alive in Christ, even from the foundation of the world; if not so, God is a partial God, and also a changeable God, and a respecter of persons; for how many little children have died without baptism!

"Wherefore, if little children could not be saved without baptism, these must have gone to an endless hell.

"Behold I say unto you, that he that supposeth that little children need baptism is in the gall of bitterness and in the bonds of iniquity, for he hath neither faith, hope, nor charity; wherefore, should he be cut off while in the thought, he must go down to hell.

"For awful is the wickedness to suppose that God saveth one child because of baptism, and the other must perish because he hath no baptism.

"Wo be unto them that shall pervert the ways of the Lord after this manner, for they shall perish except they repent. Behold, I speak with boldness, having authority from God; and I fear not what man can do; for perfect love casteth out all fear.

"And I am filled with charity, which is everlasting love; wherefore, all children are alike unto me; wherefore, I love little children with a perfect love; and they are alike and partakers of salvation.

"For I know that God is not a partial God, neither

a changeable being; but he is unchangeable from all eternity to all eternity.

"Little children cannot repent; wherefore, it is awful wickedness to deny the pure mercies of God unto them, for they are all alike in him because of his mercy.

"And he that saith that little children need baptism denieth the mercies of Christ, and setteth at naught the atonement of him and the power of his redemption.

"Wo unto such, for they are in danger of death, hell, and an endless torment. I speak it boldly; God hath commanded me. Listen unto them and give heed, or they stand against you at the judgment-seat of Christ.

"For behold that all little children are alive in Christ, and also all they that are without the law. For the power of redemption cometh on all them that have no law; wherefore, he that is not condemned, or he that is under no condemnation, cannot repent; and unto such baptism availeth nothing—

"But it is mockery before God, denying the mercies of Christ, and the power of his Holy Spirit, and putting trust in dead works.

"Behold, my son, this thing ought not to be; for repentance is unto them that are under condemnation and under the curse of a broken law.

"And the first fruits of repentance is baptism; and baptism cometh by faith unto the fulfilling the commandments; and the fulfilling the commandments bringeth remission of sins;

"And the remission of sins bringeth meekness, and lowliness of heart; and because of meekness and lowliness of heart cometh the visitation of the Holy Ghost, which Comforter filleth with hope and perfect love, which love endureth by diligence unto prayer, until the end shall come, when all the saints shall dwell with God." (Moroni 8:2-26.)

Chapter Ten

THE HOLY TRINITY

Brigham Young taught that Adam, or Michael, assisted the Deity in the creation of the world. He said: "It is true that the earth was organized by three distinct characters, namely, Elohim, Yahovah and Michael, these three forming a quorum." Then he distinguished these three from the Holy Trinity, as he spoke in the same paragraph defining "the Deity as Father, Son, and Holy Ghost." (JD, 1:51.)

Those who endeavor to say that Adam in reality was Elohim have here the words of the very man they so love to quote — President Young — to the effect that Elohim, Yahovah, and Michael were *three distinct characters*," completely refuting the claim that Elohim and Michael (Adam) were one and the same being.

This great pioneer prophet-leader clearly distinguishes between the three who made the earth and the Deity whom he defines as Father, Son, and Holy Ghost, who make up the Holy Trinity.

We do not know what part Michael played in the creation of this earth. President Young did not make it clear. But that he did take part, President Young declares with certainty. The very fact that he did, the very fact that Elohim and Jehovah did likewise, the three working in a "quorum capacity," as President Young explains, again clears the air so far as Michael being Deity is concerned. He was not Deity. He was the Archangel working with Deity.

Modern revelation emphatically states: "Michael,

or Adam, the father of all, the prince of all, the ancient of days." (D&C 27:11.)

It is this same Michael — still an angel, never identified as Deity, but rather as the angel or servant of Deity—who shall sound the trump at the beginning of the resurrection: "But, behold, verily I say unto you, before the earth shall pass away, Michael, mine archangel, shall sound his trump, and then shall all the dead awake, for their graves shall be opened, and they shall come forth—yea, even all." (D&C 29:26.)

It therefore becomes clear beyond all question that the three who organized the earth were a separate "quorum," a different triumvirate, apart from the Holy Trinity. The entire Trinity is identified by President Young as Deity, but not so with the group that organized the earth, for one of them, Michael, was not Deity—he was still an angel, although the head of the angels.

It is interesting that President Young would speak of Adam, as Michael, assisting in the creation of the earth. It was really most appropriate that Michael should help form the earth which he was to occupy as the first man, and which would become a home for his descendants. And since the Savior, as Jehovah, was to come to this same earth to bring about the atonement for the first sin to be committed here, it likewise was most appropriate that he also take part in this earth's creation.

So both worked together in the creation, Jehovah and Michael, under the direction of the Eternal Father, Elohim. And both worked together in the over-all plan of salvation for mankind, Adam providing mortality without which we could not be tried and tested in the Lord's plan, and Jesus providing the redemption, both from mortality and its ultimate end — death — and from sin, which likewise was part of our mortal experience.

How remarkable that we learn that these two great

beings—Christ, the Son of God, and Michael, his chief servant—worked so closely and in such unity to make possible the eternal progress of human kind. As servants of the Eternal Father, they truly became the principle instruments in the Almighty's hands for bringing to pass the mortality, immortality, and eternal life of man.

It is easily understood, then, as the Prophet Joseph said, that Adam stands next to Christ in authority. (*Teachings*, p. 158.)

We do not know what part the Holy Ghost may have taken in the creation. The King James Version of the Bible says: "In the beginning God created the heaven and the earth. And the earth was without form and void, and darkness was upon the face of the deep. And the Spirit of God moved upon the face of the waters." (Genesis 1:1-2. Italics added.)

The Jerusalem Bible says: ". . . And God's spirit hovered over the water."

The Smith-Goodspeed American version does not mention it, and neither does the Torah. However, the "Holy Scriptures" according to the masoretic text, a publication of the Jewish Publication Society of America, reads: ". . . and the Spirit of God hovered over the face of the waters."

Billy Graham's version reads: ". . . the earth was at first a shapeless, chaotic mass, with the Spirit of God brooding over the dark vapors."

Our book of Moses says: "I am the Beginning and the End, the Almighty God; by mine Only Begotten I created these things; yea, in the beginning I created the heaven, and the earth upon which thou standest. And the earth was without form, and void; and I caused darkness to come up upon the face of the deep; *and my Spirit moved upon the face of the water*, for I am God." (Moses 2:1-2.)

The book of Abraham says: ". . . they, that is the Gods, organized and formed the heavens and the earth. . . . and darkness reigned upon the face of the

85

deep, and the Spirit of the Gods was brooding upon the face of the waters." (Abraham 4:1-2.)

In his *Articles of Faith*, Dr. James E. Talmage says this:

"The Holy Ghost is associated with the Father and the Son in the Godhead. In the light of revelation, we are instructed as to the distinct personality of the Holy Ghost. He is a being endowed with the attributes and powers of Deity, and not a mere force, or essence. The term Holy Ghost and its common synonyms, Spirit of God, Spirit of the Lord, or simply, Spirit, Comforter, and Spirit of Truth, occur in the scriptures with plainly different meanings, referring in some cases to the person of God the Holy Ghost, and in other instances to the power or authority of this great Personage, or to the agencies through which He ministers. The context of such passages show which of these significations applies." (P. 159.)

And then Dr. Talmage goes on to say:

"Much of the confusion existing in human conceptions concerning the nature of the Holy Ghost arises from the common failure to segregate His person and powers. Plainly, such expressions as being filled with the Holy Ghost, and His falling upon persons, have reference to the powers and influences that emanate from God, and which are characteristic of Him; for the Holy Ghost may in this way operate simultaneously upon many persons even though they be widely separated, whereas the actual person of the Holy Ghost cannot be in more than one place at a time. Yet we read that through the power of the Spirit, the Father and the Son operate in their creative acts and in their general dealings with the human family. The Holy Ghost may be regarded as the minister of the Godhead, carrying into effect the decision of the Supreme Council.

"In the execution of these great purposes, the Holy Ghost directs and controls the varied forces of nature, of which indeed a few, and these perhaps of minor order wonderful as even the least of them appears to man, have thus far been investigated by mortals. Gravitation, sound, heat, light, and the still more mysterious and seemingly supernatural power of electricity, are but the common servants of the Holy Ghost in His operations. No earnest thinker, no sincere investigator supposes that he has yet learned of all the forces existing in and operating upon matter; indeed, the observed phenomena of nature, yet wholly inexplicable to him, far outnumber those for which he has devised even a partial explanation. There are powers and forces at the command of God, compared with which electricity is as the pack-horse to the locomotive, the foot messenger to the telegraph, the raft of logs to the ocean steamer. With all his scientific knowledge man knows but little respecting the enginery of creation; and yet the few forces known to him have brought about miracles and wonders, which but for their actual realization would be beyond belief. These mighty agencies, and the mightier ones still to man unknown, and many, perhaps, to the present condition of the human mind unknowable, do not constitute the Holy Ghost, but are the agencies ordained to serve His purposes." (Pages 160-61.)

As Dr. Talmage explains, there is a difference between the personage of the Holy Ghost and the power that he directs and by which such great things are accomplished.

Certainly the Spirit of God was operative in some way in the creation. Some verses in section 88 of the Doctrine and Covenants are interesting in this regard. After the Lord refers to the Holy Spirit or the Comforter, he speaks of the truth which shineth: "This is the light of Christ. As also he is in the sun, and the light of the sun, and the power thereof by which it was made.

"As also he is in the moon, and is the light of the moon, and the power thereof by which it was made;

"As also the light of the stars, and the power thereof by which they were made;

"And the earth also, and the power thereof, even the earth upon which you stand. . . .

"Which light proceedeth forth from the presence of God to fill the immensity of space—

"The light which is in all things, which giveth light to all things, which is the law by which all things are governed, even the power of God who sitteth upon his throne, who is in the bosom of eternity, who is in the midst of all things." (D&C 88:7-10, 12-13.)

And then he says:

"All kingdoms have a law given,

"And there are many kingdoms, for there is no space in the which there is no kingdom, and there is no kingdom in which there is no space, either a greater or a lesser kingdom.

"And unto every kingdom is given a law; and unto every law there are certain bounds also and conditions." (D&C 88:36-38.)

Chapter Eleven

THE REDEMPTION

"For as in Adam all die, even so in Christ shall all be made alive," the apostle Paul told the Corinthians, as in one sentence he summarized both the fall and the atonement. (1 Corinthians 15:22.)

Jesus was the "Lamb slain from the foundation of the world," and accepted the position of Redeemer in the preexistence at the great council in heaven held in the presence of the Father. How noble, how great was Jehovah as he said in that primeval council: "Father, thy will be done, and the glory be thine forever." (Moses 4:2.)

In discussing the fall and the atonement, the prophet Moroni testified:

"But behold, I will show unto you a God of miracles, even the God of Abraham, and the God of Isaac, and the God of Jacob; and it is that same God who created the heavens and the earth, and all things that in them are.

"Behold he created Adam, and by Adam came the fall of man. And because of the fall of man came Jesus Christ, even the Father and the Son; and because of Jesus Christ came the redemption of man.

"And because of the redemption of man, which came by Jesus Christ, they are brought back into the presence of the Lord; yea, this is wherein all men are redeemed, because the death of Christ bringeth to pass the resurrection, which bringeth to pass a redemption from an endless sleep, from which sleep all men shall be awakened by the power of God when the trump shall sound; and they shall come forth, both small and great, and all shall stand before his bar, being redeemed and loosed from this eternal band of death, which death is a temporal death.

"And then cometh the judgment of the Holy One upon them; and then cometh the time that he that is filthy shall be filthy still; and he that is righteous shall be righteous still; he that is happy shall be happy still; and he that is unhappy shall be unhappy still." (Mormon 9:11-14.)

The prophet Jacob, in the Book of Mormon, said:

"O the greatness of the mercy of our God, the Holy One of Israel! For he delivereth his saints from that awful monster the devil, and death, and hell, and that lake of fire and brimstone, which is endless torment.

"O how great the holiness of our God! For he knoweth all things, and there is not anything save he knows it.

"And he cometh into the world that he may save all men if they will hearken unto his voice; for behold, he suffereth the pains of all men, yea, the pains of every living creature, both men, women, and children, who belong to the family of Adam.

"And he suffereth this that the resurrection might pass upon all men, that all might stand before him at the great and judgment day.

"And he commandeth all men that they must repent, and be baptized in his name, having perfect faith in the Holy One of Israel, or they cannot be saved in the kingdom of God.

"And if they will not repent and believe in his name, and be baptized in his name, and endure to the end, they must be damned; for the Lord God, the Holy One of Israel, has spoken it.

"Wherefore, he has given a law; and where there is no law given there is no punishment; and where there is no punishment there is no condemnation; and where there is no condemnation the mercies of the Holy One of Israel have claim upon them, because of the atonement; for they are delivered by the power of him.

"For the atonement satisfieth the demands of his justice upon all those who have not the law given to them, that they are delivered from that awful monster, death and hell, and the devil, and the lake of fire and brimstone, which is endless torment; and they are restored to that God who gave them breath, which is the Holy One of Israel.

"But wo unto him that has the law given, yea, that has all the commandments of God, like unto us, and that transgresseth them, and that wasteth the days of his probation, for awful is his state!

"O that cunning plan of the evil one! O the vainness, and the frailties, and the foolishness of men! When they are learned they think they are wise, and they hearken not unto the counsel of God, for they set it aside, supposing they know of themselves, wherefore, their wisdom is foolishness and it profiteth them not. And they shall perish.

"But to be learned is good if they hearken unto the counsels of God." (2 Nephi 9:19-29.)

These words of the Savior are significant:

"As the Father knoweth me, even so know I the Father: and I lay down my life for the sheep.

"And other sheep I have which are not of this fold; them also I must bring, and they shall hear my voice; and there shall be one fold, and one shepherd.

"Therefore doth my Father love me, because I lay down my life, that I might take it again.

"No man taketh it from me, but I lay it down myself. I have power to lay it down, and I have power to take it again. This commandment have I received of my Father." (John 10:15-18.)

And one of the greatest things we have on the atonement is a revelation given through Joseph Smith in which the Savior said:

"Wherefore, I command you to repent, and keep the commandments which you have received by the hand of my servant Joseph Smith, Jun., in my name:

"And it is by my almighty power that you have received them;

"Therefore I command you to repent—repent, lest I smite you by the rod of my mouth, and by my wrath, and by my anger, and your sufferings be sore—how sore you know not, how exquisite you know not, yea, how hard to bear you know not.

"For behold, I, God, have suffered these things for all, that they might not suffer if they would repent;

"But if they would not repent they must suffer even as I;

"Which suffering caused myself, even God, the greatest of all, to tremble because of pain, and to bleed at every pore, and to suffer both body and spirit—and would that I might not drink the bitter cup, and shrink—

"Nevertheless, glory be to the Father, and I partook and finished my preparations unto the children of men.

"Wherefore, I command you again to repent, lest I humble you with my almighty power; and that you confess your sins, lest you suffer these punishments of which I have spoken, of which in the smallest, yea, even in the least degree you have tasted at the time I withdrew my Spirit." (D&C 19:13-20.)

And then he concludes:

"Pray always, and I will pour out my Spirit upon you, and great shall be your blessing—yea, even more than if you should obtain treasures of earth and corruptibleness to the extent thereof.

"Behold, canst thou read this without rejoicing and lifting up thy heart for gladness?

"Or canst thou run about longer as a blind guide?

"Or canst thou be humble and meek, and conduct thyself wisely before me? Yea, come unto me thy Savior. Amen." (D&C 19:38-41.)

INDEX

through fall of Adam, 5

Evolution, taught in schools, 43; statements of scientists concerning, 43-47

Evolutionists, discoveries of, 39; admit evidence is conjectural, 49-50

Exaltation, made possible through fall of Adam, 5; through Jesus Christ, 14

Eyring, Dr. Henry, on the creation, 41-42

Fall, of Adam and Eve was necessary, 4; Adam's, a basic foundation of the gospel, 26-27; account of, in Book of Mormon, 29-30; Bible accounts of, 69-72; Joseph Fielding Smith regarding the, 74-77

First Presidency, Adam holds keys of, 58,60

Fisk, Dr. Alfred G., on evolution, 44-45

Fleming, Ambrose, on the creation, 39

Forgiveness, of Adam, 60-61

Fraser-Harris, on the creation, 40

Free agency, essential to gospel of Christ, 62-63

Garden of Eden, considered a myth, 1; temptation in, 4

Genealogy, of the Savior, 5, 59; was kept by early man, 57

Geneticist, on evolution, 43-44

Gladstone, William, on the Bible, 37

God, Adam and Eve were children of, 5; performed marriage of Adam and Eve, 5; Adam is not, 14-15, 61; Adam could become like unto a, 21

Goodspeed Bible, 21

Gospel, preached in the preexistence, 64-65

Gospel Kingdom, the, 19

Greeley, Horace, on the Bible, 38

Hathaway, Dr.Claude M., on the creation, 40-41

Holy Ghost, in creation, 85-86; nature of, 86-87

Holy Trinity, not same as group that organized earth, 83-84

Infants, who die before baptism,

3; Mormon, on baptism of, 80-82

Intelligence, of Adam, 54-55, 57-58

Israelites, 2

Jacob, on the atonement, 90-91

Jeans, James, on the creation, 39-40

Jerusalem Bible, 69,70,85

Jesus Christ, exaltation through, 14; physical appearance of, 53

Jewish Book of Knowledge, 2

Jewish race, survival of, aided by Bible, 36

Jewish scholars say Bible accounts are myths, 1

Journal of Discourses, Brigham Young misquoted in, 16-19

Kant, Immanuel, on the Bible, 37

Knox Catholic Bible, 21, 71

Lammerts, Dr. Walter Edward, on evolution, 43-44

Latter-day Saint, beliefs of a, concerning Adam and Eve, 25-27; beliefs of a, concerning Bible, 36

Lexicographers' interpretation of Adam and Eve, 2

Libby, Dr. W. F., developed radiocarbon "time clock," 48-49

Life, age of, upon earth, 47-49

Lincoln, Abraham, on Bible, 37

Living Bible, 69,71,85

Lord, gives commandments to Adam and Eve, 4

Luce, Clare Booth, 46

Lucifer, ejected from heaven by Adam, 8-10; was an angel, 9

Man, physical image of, 53

Man Does Not Stand Alone, 46-47

Marriage of Adam and Eve, 5-6

Mather, Kirtley F., on creation, 45

Michael, Adam known as, 7; has great ministry related to latter days, 10-11; assisted in creation, 13, 83

Millenial Star, sermon of Brigham Young not published in, 17-18

Millikan, Robert, on atheism, 45

Misconceptions concerning first parents, 1